DEBUNKING THE MIDDLE-CLASS MYTH

Why Diverse Schools Are Good for All Kids

Eileen Gale Kugler

A SCARECROWEDUCATION BOOK

The Scarecrow Press, Inc.
Lanham, Maryland, and Oxford
2002

A ScarecrowEducation Book

Published in the United States of America
by Scarecrow Press, Inc.
A Member of the Rowman & Littlefield Publishing Group
4720 Boston Way, Lanham, Maryland 20706
www.scaroweducation.com

PO Box 317
Oxford
OX2 9RU, UK

Illustrations: "Freedom," by Trong Nguyen, p. iv; "Self-Portrait and Friend,"
by Ji Kim, p. 1; "Face," by Mohamed Elmubarak, p. 45; "Jazz Club," by Julia
Ehrenfeld, p. 81; "Christmas Deer," by Dennis Bundu, p. 150

British Library Cataloguing in Publication Information Available

Library of Congress Cataloging-in-Publication Data

Kugler, Eileen Gale, 1950–
  Debunking the middle-class myth : why diverse schools are good for all
kids / Eileen Gale Kugler.
      p. cm.
"A ScarecrowEducation book."
Includes bibliographical references (p.).
  ISBN 0-8108-4511-3 (hardcover : alk. paper) — ISBN 0-8108-4512-1
(pbk. : alk. paper)
  1. Multicultural education—United States. I. Title.
  LC1099.3 .K84 2002
  370.117'0973—dc21

                                                        2002008700

♾™ The paper used in this publication meets the minimum requirements of
American National Standard for Information Sciences—Permanence of Paper
for Printed Library Materials, ANSI/NISO Z39.48-1992.
Manufactured in the United States of America.

To my husband, Larry, a dedicated educator and
my true partner in everything important in my life

and

To Annandale High Principals Donald Clausen and Ray Watson
who made me sorry I had only two children to send to their
remarkable school.

"Freedom," by Trong Nguyen

CONTENTS

FOREWORD

By Gary Orfield
Codirector, Civil Rights Project
Professor of Education and Social Policy, Harvard University

We are a multiracial nation rapidly approaching the day when there will be no racial majority group in the nation's schools. That can be one of our country's greatest strengths. Yet, in too many neighborhoods and too many schools, these races and cultures are segregated, largely ignorant, and too often fearful of each other. Housing remains seriously segregated, separating people by race and economic status. Our schools—where children are taught about our society both in the classroom and in learning from other students—increasingly isolate our children, despite the U.S. Supreme Court ruling some fifty years ago that segregated schools are "inherently unequal."

But there are thousands of schools that successfully bring together students from many races and ethnicities. These diverse schools offer our young people the matchless opportunity of learning and playing and talking with others who can broaden their own life experiences. Students of all backgrounds in these schools benefit from enriched discussions, leading to better understanding of diverse points of view. These students learn how to work with people from varying races and ethnic groups, skills that will be invaluable in their adult lives. In surveys we are carrying out in schools in many parts of the country, students of all races report such experiences.

Integrated schools, however, are often maligned. They are misjudged and misunderstood by people who know little about what actually takes place in their classrooms and hallways, adults still possessed by the stereotypes and fears of their own childhood. For years, much of white society has idealized the segregated middle-class suburban white school with beautiful facilities and children from affluent white families, assuming this is the place where students receive the best education. Realtors further this perspective publishing the test scores and college-enrollment rates from such schools. But this disregards what we know about the value of going to school with students from different races and cultures. A school with a diverse student body provides benefits to students across racial and ethnic lines, benefits that aren't available in a segregated environment, benefits that prepare students to function much more effectively in the interracial colleges, workplaces, and communities of our future.

Eileen Kugler, whose children have experienced an exceptionally diverse school in the midst of one the nation's largest suburban systems, challenges the misconceptions about diverse schools head on. From her years of experience as a parent and then as a community leader, she heard the myths, and she witnessed the truth. She listened to others from around the country as they told similar stories about often unnoticed but significant successes in their schools. In this book, she debunks the myths about diverse schools, illustrating with firsthand accounts and poignant stories what we in the research community have been finding from surveys and statistical studies. This book will help educators, students, parents, community leaders, and policy makers to better understand the opportunities in diverse schools and how to realize them.

I have taught students from all corners of the country in five of the nation's great research universities—Harvard, Princeton, University of Virginia, University of Chicago, University of Illinois. I have consistently found that students who have lived and been educated in diverse communities have a much richer and more sophisticated understanding of our society and are far more comfortable in working with students from other backgrounds. Certainly they write vastly more interesting essays for college admissions. I think that parents should consider whether they are helping or hurting their children when they take them from settings where they can develop these skills and understandings to places where they cannot. My own children went to diverse schools in Washington, D.C., Chicago, Champaign, Ill., and Cambridge, Mass. Each of them has had great success in college and professional school, and each has a kind of comfort and understanding across racial lines that has enriched their lives and ours with friends and understanding.

Many Americans know that it is important for our children to understand and feel comfortable in the diverse society in which their lives will unfold—more than nine-tenths in one recent national survey—but they do nothing to give their children the experience, often fleeing from racial diversity. Both for individuals and for policy makers, this book should be thought provoking.

Listen to the story of the strengths of diverse schools told from the perspective of a parent who reports the gifts diversity bestowed upon her children, herself, and her entire community. This is an important story of hope in a time in which too many dreams are being abandoned and too many divisions are deepening. It argues that inside of what is often seen as a problem is an opportunity for all children to gain academically and to learn to live and work together in ways that can enrich their lives and their community's future. It turns out that our children do not know why they can't do this, and that they and their teachers can find ways to make this succeed if given half a chance. It turns out to be fascinating and deeply hopeful.

Maybe the dreamers were right and the demagogues wrong. Readers living in diverse communities will find much to help them here; those who have been told that they should raise their children in segregated white communities will find something to think seriously about.

PREFACE

I am a middle-class white woman. For a long time, I felt I did not have the standing to write a book about diversity. But, after long conversations and much soul searching, I came to realize my perspective is not only valid, it's critical.

I am a middle-class white woman whose two children attended one of the most diverse public high schools in the country, Annandale High in Fairfax County, Virginia, and I am deeply grateful that they had the opportunity to be educated in this remarkable school. I watched parents of younger children move out of our school district as they fell victim to negative myths about schools with a broad mix of racial, ethnic, and socioeconomic backgrounds. At the same time, I watched my children flourish both academically and socially. Both went on to excel at top national colleges, and both feel "privileged" (their word) to have been a part of their multicultural public high school.

Today, my children are comfortable in any environment, talking to just about anyone. And they know how to listen and how to respect opinions that are different from their own, growing from the exposure.

I have read much of the recent research on diverse schools, and it has been gratifying for me to see the conclusions that I have drawn from my personal experiences borne out in studies from prestigious institutions.[1]

But truthfully, this book didn't stem from major academic research. It was inspired by own observations of my children, and other people's children, and of teachers, administrators, and community leaders—all touched by an incredible school. All who allowed themselves to be a part of Annandale High were transformed by the experience. We all grew exponentially and became educated in the best sense of the word. I would not have wanted my children to be in any other school, regardless of tuition or location.

My passion for the benefits of an education in a diverse school has led me to speak and write about the strengths of these schools, and to work with communities to develop strategies that build support for them. I've talked with many parents, students, and educators, and I have heard that same passion about the learning environment expressed over and over again. There is overwhelming enthusiasm for what these schools have to offer. And there is overwhelming frustration at the misinformation that abounds among those who don't have firsthand experience with a diverse school.

This story needs to be told. We need to share the lessons learned from these remarkable places. We need to spread this information so that middle-class parents—parents who have the luxury to choose their neighborhoods—stop falling for the negative myths that lead them to move into neighborhoods where everyone looks and thinks alike. We need to encourage these parents to seek out schools where children of various backgrounds enrich academics and social interactions by bringing a range of experiences and knowledge to the classroom, because that is simply the best way to educate all children.

I was fortunate enough to be associated with a diverse school that has had extraordinary leadership. I worked with two skilled, caring principals, both of them truly the right men for the job at the right time. I watched Ray Watson lead the school through the turbulence of its "wake-up call," steadfastly guiding it from the tension of a rapidly diversifying student body to the enthusiasm of a school community united in its commitment to reap the benefits of its diversity. I then watched Don Clausen build on this foundation to help faculty and students reach new heights as a world-class educational institution, touted in national media.

As enriching as diverse schools can be, they can only reach their potential if they have leadership that enthusiastically takes on the challenge of making them successful.

This book shows the results when educators are committed to finding ways to help every child, of every background, succeed. And it shows what is possible when all elements of the community—students, parents, and community members—support the administration and teachers in their efforts.

This book lays out the rationale for considering diverse schools among the most desirable; and it provides strategies for anyone who cares about strengthening these often underrated treasures in our educational system. A diverse school that is well run and supported by the community is an academic and social gold mine. It provides just the type of education that our students and our greater society need.

From everything I've been told, this perspective has not been articulated through the eyes of a parent, yet it is genuinely shared by thousands of parents and educators across the country. I've been encouraged repeatedly to tell this story, and to tell it loudly.

To fully articulate my message, I must be clear on how "diverse schools" are defined in this book. I feel strongly that the term "diverse" has been increasingly misused to mean any place with minority students. I used it as the word is defined in other contexts, to mean a varied mix. Thus, a diverse school has a population of students from a variety of races and cultures. A school that is 98 percent African American or Mexican American is no more diverse than one that is 98 percent Caucasian. In seeking people to interview for the book, I tried to identify schools with populations that were not only diverse racially and ethnically but also socioeconomically, because that is a critical factor in creating a truly diverse environment. These schools do exist and there would be more of them if middle-class, particularly white, families did not flee from school districts with increasing diversity.

I hope this book raises the level of discussion at universities, think tanks, school buildings, and dinner tables. However, I make no claim that it represents an academic research document. It recounts a personal journey, bolstered by the experiences of many others around the nation with personal connections to diverse schools.

My goal is to encourage parents of every economic status and every race or culture to seek out well-run diverse public schools, enjoy their benefits, and help to make them work. I hope it will inspire competent educators to flock to these schools and work to provide all students with what they need to achieve. And I hope entire communities will rally around these precious gems in their midst. I can assure you that when it all comes together, the results are extraordinary.

The experience of being part of a school like Annandale High School can't be bought or measured on standardized tests. It is beyond value or measurement and it will be in your heart for a lifetime.

NOTE

1. For an excellent summary of the research supporting the benefits of education in a diverse environment, see Gary Orfield, ed., *Diversity Challenged* (Cambridge, Mass.: Harvard Education Publishing Group, 2001).

ACKNOWLEDGMENTS

This book has been a labor of love. Few people get to combine their professional life with their passion, and I appreciate this glorious opportunity.

I am grateful to Maggie Bedrosian and Lynne Waymon for their early advice on how to turn my experiences into a book worth reading.

The book would never have been envisioned, let alone written, if I did not have the extraordinary fortune of being an active part of the Annandale High School community. I thank former Principal Ray Watson for welcoming me into his office as a collaborator within twelve hours of my volunteering! He led Annandale High during a crucial period of transition and provided the type of leadership that it deserved.

My unending respect, admiration, and thanks to Annandale Principal Don Clausen, who allowed me to volunteer by his side for many years as the school set new goals and strived to reach them every day. I am grateful for his commitment to the education of each child, his openness to new ideas, and his willingness to truly make parents partners in their children's education. Annandale High is indeed fortunate to have this ethical, caring, professional leader at its helm.

The artwork that enlivens the cover and pages of the book was produced by some of the wonderful students at Annandale High. I am grateful to artists Trong Nguyen, Ji Kim, Mohamed Elmubarak, Julia Ehrenfeld, and Dennis Bundu for letting me showcase their works on the inside of the book. Art teacher Joyce Weinstein, a talented artist whose work is shown internationally, was instrumental in guiding these young artists and pulling together these remarkable pieces for the book. As always, she went to great lengths to help her students receive the recognition they deserve. Lejia Lombardi did a beautiful job photographing these works for publication, with the support of her teacher Scott Saylor.

My thanks to the Annandale High community would not be complete without acknowledging the wonderful parents who have worked with me in the trenches of parent involvement, inspiring me every time we get together. Annandale is fortunate to have many dedicated parent leaders who spend countless hours working to improve the education of every child at the school. In particular, I would like to thank Susan Collins, Liz Segall, Jennifer Van Pernis, Andrea Sobel, and Judy Miller for carrying the mantle of parent leadership so admirably.

And of course, I must thank the teachers of Annandale High who taught my children and many others with caring, enthusiasm, and creativity. They also welcomed parent input and support. My years as a parent leader at Annandale High were made worthwhile by the many, many teachers who went out of their way to personally thank me for my involvement. This is my thanks to them for the commitment they show on a daily basis.

Thanks to many in the leadership of Fairfax County Public Schools (FCPS) for supporting my efforts in writing this book, as well as involvement during the years that led to its development. Superintendent Dan Domenech has been approachable, helpful, and supportive at every turn. I also want to thank Kitty Porterfield and Paul Regnier of the Office of Community Relations for many collaborative efforts.

Brenda Greene of the National School Board Association (NSBA), a colleague on the FCPS Superintendent's Community Advisory Council, was with me when the embryo of my book was first given life. I am grateful for her continuing help as well as others at NSBA, including Edwin Darden, Dottie Gray, and Mike Wessley. I also appreciate the time spent with me by Gary Orfield and his colleagues Pedro Noguera and Jimmy Kim of the Harvard Civil Rights Project; Arnie Fege of the

Public Education Network; Anne Henderson, a senior consultant to New York University's Institute of Education and Social Policy; Marty Blank of the Institute for Educational Leadership and its affiliated Communities in Schools; Alan Berube of the Brookings Institute; Richard Kahlenberg of the Twentieth Century Fund; Holly Kreider of Harvard's Family Involvement Network of Educators; and Jay Matthews of the *Washington Post*.

The person most responsible for helping take me from enthusiastic concept to cohesive book was Tom Koerner of ScarecrowEducation. He was always encouraging and supportive. I also appreciate the work of editor Jessica McCleary in competently shepherding the book through the publication process.

I am fortunate to have had excellent help in pulling this book together. Ellen Johnson has been a treasured colleague on many projects, and her help was again of great value to me. Laurie Aomarie provided competent assistance at a crucial point. Jan Prince worked with me in the final hours, giving me valuable insights, helpful production support, and energy when my supply was exhausted. Teacher Randi Adleberg, a friend who agreed to read the manuscript when she had much other pressing business, provided thoughtful comments and wonderful suggestions. If you like the student artwork showcased in this book as much as I do, you can thank Randi for giving me the idea!

Many educational leaders, teachers, students, parents, and community members from diverse school communities willingly gave their time to discuss the issues of this book with me. Their insights make the pages of this book come alive. They include Susan Akroyd, Erin Albright, Anne Alpert, Jamilah Alzer, Kate Andreatta, Jamie Bacigalupi, Lori Barb, Mary Barter, Beverley Baxter, Alex Berens, Cathy Belter, Kate Bradley, Diane Brody, Ben Bushman, Kelly Butler, Taylor Butler, Isis Castro, Joe Cirasuolo, Susan Collins, Virginia Crowley, Sunny Day, Alice Donlan, Tom Donlan, Nancy Doorey, Donna Erickson, Jennifer Finney, Mollie Fox, David Freeman, Yvonne Freeman, Gil Garcia, Susie Gaskins, Libia Gil, Sharon Greenbaum, Anne Henderson, Mimi Hoffman, Jo Anne Hughes, Katharine Johnson, Geraldine Kearns, Lynne Kielhorn, Jeri Kitner, Susan Klaw, Juli Kwikkel, Joe Light, Harriet Ann Litwin, Mary Mason, Winnie McGarty, Leila Meyerratken, Vic Meyers, Don Montoya, Cliff Moon, Ayobamidele

Odejimi, Betty Paschall, Jan Patton, Stan Paz, Melanie Pethcry, Tom Pratuch, Mark Prosser, Jane Rice, Danni Rumber, Donna Schutz, Liz Segall, Andy Shallal, Mark Shugoll, Merrill Shugoll, Roni Silverstein, Debbie Simons, Jaspreet Singh, Nathan Sisterson, Andrea Sobel, Amy Spencer, Brian Straughter, Carolyn Tabarini, Grace Taylor, Trish Tripepi, Gladys Vaccarezza, Jennifer Van Pernis, Joyce Weinstein, Alan Weintraut, and Eleanor Woodard.

And saving the best for last, I must thank my family. I thank my parents for giving me the self-confidence to believe I could do anything I set my mind to and for cheering me on at every step. And I thank my mother-in-law for the enthusiasm she showed for all the good things that came my way, including the contract for the book. I am truly sorry she is not here to see it published.

My terrific kids, Sara and Alex, were the motivating force behind this book. How could I not support a school that nurtured the best in them and helped them become the caring individuals and broad thinkers they are? I thank them for always challenging me to reach even higher in my thinking and my actions. And I appreciate the opportunity to get to know their fascinating friends who have greatly enriched my life.

There would be no book without my husband, my high school sweetheart, my soulmate, Larry. He has spent his adult life tirelessly working to ensure that each child has the opportunities to be educated at the highest level. His genuine love and respect of all children, no matter what their background, remains an inspiration. Larry has always supported my efforts, but particularly so as I wrote this book, which sometimes took over my life (and sometimes his, as well). As with everything else in my life, Larry was a true partner.

INTRODUCTION

(W)e no longer can think of some students as void of any dignity and worth simply because they do not conform to our conventional image. All students of all backgrounds bring talents and strengths to their learning and as educators we need to find ways to build on these.

—Sonia Nieto, "What Does It Mean to Affirm Diversity?"[1]

It happens every year. Well-meaning parents begin their exploration for a new home, a place where their kids can attend a "good" school. And what's usually their primary tool for measuring a school's worth? They look at the school's standardized test scores, assuming the highest average scores definitively mean the best schools. They check out demographic statistics, fearing that high populations of minority students translate to schools where gangs rule, violence is common, and expectations are low. Far too often, they don't dig beyond the most basic statistics. They never learn that many diverse schools have challenging curricula, high-achieving graduates, and low rates of violence. The parents never investigate research that clearly shows the benefit of being educated in a diverse environment.

Who loses in the end? We all do. Gary Orfield at Harvard's Civil Rights Project has found an alarming trend toward resegregation of our schools, even though our nation's school-age population is becoming increasingly diverse.[2] One of the reasons is that parents with the economic luxury of moving into the neighborhood of their choice select predominantly white neighborhoods that feed into schools where the vast majority of students look and think alike. The escalating separation of our races and ethnic groups by school raises serious concerns.

Our nation's workforce is becoming more diverse and will continue to do so. Our students must learn how to interact with people different than they are—whether as leader, staff, seller, or buyer. This becomes even more significant as our economy becomes more international in scope.

Not only must our students learn how to function in a diverse, global marketplace, they must be educated participants in our global society. There are serious implications for assuming there is only one lens for viewing history and the events of today. On September 11, 2001, we learned that people who view the world far differently can take actions that have dramatic impacts on our daily lives in the United States. To be able to appreciate what is happening in our country and understand events in a world context, students must be exposed to people of different experiences and different frames of reference.[3]

Within the borders of the United States, we've learned difficult lessons about our traditional definition of a "good" school, basically a school where middle-class kids score high on standardized tests. Shooting rampages by disaffected teenagers have taught us that a predominantly white middle-class school with high test scores can be missing out on crucial lessons in character and respect for individual differences. What can high SAT scores tell you about a positive school climate?

Schools with diverse student populations constantly battle myths that these schools are less desirable. The reality is that a diverse school can provide a first-class academic education. Learning comes alive when wisdom is shared not only by competent teachers and textbooks, but also by fellow students with life experiences and cultures that illuminate whole new worlds. With a teacher who encourages all students to speak their minds and listen to others, classroom discussions with students from varying backgrounds are rich and challenging, fostering critical thinking skills. Students learn there is a range of perspectives on issues, motivating them to study and thoughtfully define their own views. These schools provide world-class academic environments.

Beyond valuable academic lessons, diverse schools offer unique op-portunities to learn significant life skills. Dangerous stereotypes break down as students study, play ball, and just talk with one another. The seeds of tolerance and respect are planted and bred in schools with stu-dents from all over the world.

A well-run school will seize each of these opportunities and build a solid school community where every student, parent, educator, and community member benefits. Many parents, including white parents like myself, would never trade this for a homogenous environment where our children's world is limited to those who look and think like they do. I want my children's world expanded, not boxed in.

My inspiration for writing this book came from my decade-plus in-volvement with a school that championed its extreme diversity, Annan-dale High in Fairfax County, Virginia, a few miles outside of Washington, D.C. The academic and personal growth of my children was staggering in this school with students hailing from more than eighty-five countries, speaking more than forty native languages. Not only is this school diverse ethnically and racially, students also come from wide-ranging economic backgrounds—from those who share bedrooms with siblings and cousins to those who live in $600,000 homes, and every income level in between. I can't imagine a religion not represented, with the halls filled with stu-dents wearing Christian crosses or Jewish Stars of David, along with Muslim girls wearing *hijabs* covering their heads, Sikh boys with their hair wrapped in turbans, and Hindi girls in traditional saris. Hairstyles range from carefully crafted cornrows to a young athlete's microscopic buzz. I felt drawn into the magnetic pull of this ethnic and cultural gold mine, every day feeling fortunate that my whole family could learn from these young minds with so much to share.

Annandale High today enjoys strong community support. That is the result of many years of administrators and faculty working collabora-tively with parents and community leaders to strengthen the school and reach out to our broader community. It was not an easy path for this school that had to weather a rapidly changing student population.

Annandale High School opened its doors in 1954 in a burgeoning middle-class suburb of Washington, D.C., in the still segregated school system of Fairfax County, Virginia. In the next few decades, while seg-regation was no longer the official policy, the student population remained almost exclusively middle-class white. The school was known for its academic prowess and its state football champions.

The faces in the halls of Annandale High changed dramatically in the '80s and '90s with an increasing influx of immigrants to the area, plus a school redistricting that magnified the change. The new students were not the children of diplomats. They were largely the sons and daughters of families fleeing war-torn countries, failing economies, and religious or ethnic prejudice. In short, they are the type of immigrants that have been the foundation of the United States for decades.

The school had some tough times as faculty and students struggled with how to deal with the new reality. Fights broke out along racial lines, and the school administration quickly realized that the evolving school population required a new leadership paradigm. With the support of the school board and superintendent, Annandale's principal and faculty took on the task of building a model diverse school, where every student is challenged and helped to flourish academically, and the lessons of respect and caring are ingrained in the fabric of the school.

The intensive efforts have paid off in countless ways. In recent years, Annandale has received national recognition for its successes, including a visit from the President's Blue Ribbon Panel on Race Relations, as well as favorable coverage in *USA Today*, on National Public Radio, and on ABC's *Good Morning America*.

Even as the school was making great strides, however, community members did not always get the message. As often happens when minority populations increase, some homeowners left the neighborhoods for "whiter" pastures. Negative stereotypes about the recent immigrants were whispered over backyard fences and around the neighborhood pools. Older residents decried the changes to their school, which no longer looked like it did when their children attended.

Despite the myths and the forces that spread them, many homeowners did remain to fight to keep the community whole, fully recognizing the potential in their community and their school. As I became involved with Annandale High, I quickly saw that public grumblings about the school were far from the reality of what went on in the classrooms of my children. Whenever I heard something negative about the school, I began asking where they heard it. I was shocked at what I found. In virtually every case, the negative comments originated with people who had nothing to do with the school. The negative comments were coming from people whose children graduated from the school decades earlier when it was all white or from parents of children in predominantly white schools. They were simply spreading the prevailing myths. On the other hand, people who got their information from someone who had firsthand knowledge of Annandale High, be it students, teachers, or parents, heard a completely different message.

As a communications consultant, I was thunderstruck by this finding. I became convinced that the way to build community support for the school was to bring firsthand knowledge of the school to those who needed to hear it, primarily those with younger children who were listening to misinformation and were moving out of the area. I led a series of meetings in each of the twelve elementary and middle schools that feed into our high school, cosponsored by the PTAs of the high school and of the primary or middle school that hosted the meeting. The high school brought a panel of administrators and teachers, along with parents and students from that neighborhood who had attended the host school. We were scrupulously honest in presenting information about the high school, never sugar-coating the truth. But the truth was so powerful and eye opening that those who came to the meetings became ardent supporters of the high school.

After every meeting, parents of younger children came up to me and asked how they could help the high school. We asked for one thing—change the dialogue over the backyard fence and around the swimming pool. Take personal responsibility to make sure myths are debunked and only accurate information is spread.

Years later, I am often greeted by parents who attended one of our outreach meetings. They share a common story. "We were about to move out of the neighborhood because of what we had heard about the high school, but after that meeting we knew we should stay. I can't thank you enough because my child is so happy here!" yet another mother recently told me.

We still fight battles of misinformation, constantly offering facts to counteract the myths. We are in frequent contact with real estate agents who say they show no preferences to schools, yet list "good schools" in a home ad only when the house feeds into predominantly white schools. In some nearby communities facing the same challenges, real estate ads have been even more troubling. One controversial ad aimed at middle-class families in an increasingly diverse area cried: "Mount Vernon schools got you down? Move!" In our neighborhood, real estate agents can price a home that feeds into Annandale High $10,000 lower than an identical one across the street that feeds into a predominantly white high school.

Yet those of us who have embraced the Annandale community and other neighborhoods like it are reminded on a daily basis what a gift these diverse schools can be to our children. I find it ironic that so many parents who are truly looking for the best education for their child steer away from these enriching environments.

I do recognize that diverse demographics alone don't make a positive educational institution, and in fact, can lead to the opposite. The truth is these schools present particular challenges to school leadership. This is not your baby boomer's public school and can't be run like one. If we are going to make the most of these schools, educational leaders must proceed with open eyes, celebrate the diversity, and commit themselves to serving all students at the school. Diverse schools that meet the needs of only an elite segment are doomed to failure. I had the opportunity to work along side a number of extraordinary educators who met the challenges with competence and caring. The entire community benefited from their work.

I also understand parents are motivated to send their children to private schools for a variety of reasons. I only ask that parents honestly consider why they are taking their child out of public schools. If you are looking at private schools because of rumors about the environment in the local school, I urge you to check out the school for yourself and make an evaluation based on fact. I think some parents will be amazed at how far the reality is from what's been whispered by people who truly don't know the facts. I also hope parents will reevaluate the decision to send a child to private school at various stages of the child's development. I've talked with parents who have sent their children to private school at the elementary level, for an extra dose of religious education or discipline or attention to special learning styles or other reasons, and then felt their children would gain more from the unique strengths of the public secondary school. Often the regional middle and high schools are where you find the true diverse populations.

The point is we all need honest, straightforward information about our schools to enable us to make decisions about where to live and where to send our children to school. Unfortunately, far too much of the information about diverse schools has been mired in myths, based on misperceptions and ignorance of the facts. A lot has been written about this issue in the professional publications read by educators, but little has been filtered to the general public. Hopefully this book will change that.

It's the responsibility of those of us who do know the reality to publicly debunk the myths that poison the public's perception of diverse schools. These myths lead us to make judgments that can harm our children, our families, and our society at large. We must confront them, discard them, and focus instead on the real opportunities and challenges of these schools.

NOTES

1. Sonia Nieto, "What Does It Mean to Affirm Diversity?" *School Administrator* 56, no. 5 (May 1999): 6–7.

2. Gary Orfield, *Schools More Separate: Consequences of a Decade of Resegregation* (Cambridge, Mass.: Civil Rights Project, Harvard University, 2001).

3. In an October 17, 2001, statement introducing International Education Week, November 12–16, 2001, Secretary of Education Rod Paige said, "Knowledge about the culture and language of our neighbors throughout the world is becoming increasingly important in the daily lives of all Americans. The events surrounding the terrorist attacks of September 11 underscore that point." www.ed.gov/offices/OUS/PES/endorsement-10172001.html [accessed 15 June 2002].

I

THE MYTHS THAT POISON OUR THINKING ABOUT DIVERSE SCHOOLS

"Self-Portrait and Friend," by Ji Kim

1

MYTH 1

The Best School for My Child Is the One with the Highest Standardized Test Scores

Blatant and harmful misappropriation of standardized tests for fallacious uses has been a constant of America's historical experience with standardized testing in schools. . . . Tests intended to evaluate individual achievement have been used to base unfounded conclusions of the educational quality of entire school systems.

—Peter Sacks, "Predictable Losers in Testing Schemes"[1]

I was swapping kid stories with a woman I met at a social gathering recently. When I asked her where she lived, she talked about her recent search for a larger home for her growing family. Fairfax County, the sprawling Washington, D.C., suburb where we both live, offers a variety of neighborhoods and schools. Not happy with "things I've heard about" the high school her kids would have attended (a very diverse school), she said they checked out test scores and came up with a list of the neighborhood high schools she considered acceptable for her kids. Every school on her list was predominantly white.

Discouraged that she had eliminated all the diverse schools, I made a point of noting the valuable lessons my children had learned from students of other cultures at nearby Annandale High. I must have touched a chord. The other mom began citing all of the benefits her family gained from the exposure to people of other cultures in our diverse area. I couldn't deny that even the largely white schools in Northern Virginia have a small percentage of minority students, and the entire area itself presents opportunities for exposure to other cultures. But if diversity is valuable to her, why didn't she even consider it as a factor when choosing a school?

The bottom line is that she had chosen the school for her children by the same yardstick used by the vast majority of other middle-class parents. First and foremost, she looked at test scores. Never mind that the high school her children now attend is one of largest in the state, at a time when academic research declares smaller is better.[2] Never mind that an extensive survey conducted by our school district showed parent satisfaction the highest at some of the most diverse schools, and the lowest at some of the schools she considered, including the one she chose.[3] Never mind that the statewide tests scores she considered have come under harsh criticism for measuring too many disconnected facts.[4] Never mind that she valued diversity. All that mattered was how high the school's average was on standardized tests.

While our society is clearly wedded to standardized tests, their use as the sole measure of a school's worth is fatally flawed. The superintendent of Fairfax County Schools, Daniel Domenech, argues forcefully that standardized tests provide valuable information but they were never envisioned to be the sole measure of a school's worth. A poll sponsored by the American Association of School Administrators, which Domenech has served as president, found that 63 percent of respondents did not believe that one test can accurately measure students' progress.[5]

The tests themselves are notoriously biased. A number of items will simply be answered correctly more often by students from higher socioeconomic backgrounds than those from lower backgrounds, measuring not what kids learn, but what they bring to school. For example, a sixth grade science question on one standardized achievement test requires knowledge of fresh celery, which may not be familiar to students whose families don't use celery in their culture's cooking or those who find fresh vegetables a luxury.[6] Juli Kwikkel, a principal in a highly diverse elementary school in Storm Lake, Iowa, puts it in more direct terms. She asserts that nationwide standardized tests favor students who are "white, bright, and polite." In a conversation I had with Brookings researcher Richard Kahlenberg, he noted that our country's increasing emphasis on testing is exacerbating the concern of educators, "leading middle class parents to evaluate schools with more and more precision on aggregate scores which most educators know reflect the socioeconomic status of the kids in the school, as opposed to what the school is adding to the picture."[7]

Some critics of standardized testing go further. Charging that high-stakes tests emphasize the wrong things and actually lead to less effective instruction, particularly for at-risk students, Alfie Kohn writes, "Every time we judge a school on the basis of a standardized test score . . . we unwittingly help to make our schools just a little bit worse."[8]

Diverse schools suffer from a double whammy in testing. Not only are many of their students recent immigrants whose families are struggling economically, these students are also grappling to answer questions in a new language, reflecting a new culture. Sometimes this is their third or fourth language. Many very bright students miss questions because their English isn't proficient enough or their experiences aren't "American" enough to pick up nuances in the questions.

Even students who aren't language-minority can miss the loaded cultural references in test questions created by someone who lived a life far different than theirs. Ellen Berg, a middle-school teacher in St. Louis, Missouri, kept a journal online for a middle-school reform project. Her diary entry on standardized tests expressed her frustration at the results on the state assessment for her students, who are largely minority students from poor homes.

> I am frustrated because my students showed they understood the text completely, yet most of them did poorly on the assessment simply because they did not answer in a particular way. Now I am faced with spending valuable class time teaching them how to smile and nod and give "the man" what he wants rather than spending that same time helping them become better readers and writers.[9]

SAT scores, often used to evaluate the strength of high schools, present another set of inequities. The proliferation of expensive SAT prep classes promising 100-plus point improvements links the score to the child's socioeconomic status rather than academic capacity.

The focus on test scores as a parent's exclusive decision-making factor often crosses ethnic groups and races as the family moves into the middle class. At a community event, a lawyer from a Middle Eastern country grilled me about Annandale High's test scores, as he decided whether to move his young family out of the Annandale High area, even though there is a strong and successful Middle Eastern population at the school. Korean parents at Annandale High tell me they are urged by their Korean friends to send their children to the predominantly white middle-class school a few miles from Annandale with, yes, higher average test scores, but a less vibrant Korean population. A young Korean teacher told me about his childhood in Fairfax County where his parents moved him from school to school, as they gained economic status and moved into neighborhoods with schools that were less and less diverse but had higher test scores. He found himself increasingly disconnected in class, one of a handful of nonwhite students in the classes. He missed the interchange with students from varied backgrounds, including his own.

The biggest problem with using test scores to choose a school is that *average* scores don't have any significance for how an individual child will score. The *Washington Post* analyzed test scores in Montgomery County, Maryland, for a series on education. Similar to Fairfax County, its Virginia neighbor, Montgomery has historically been an affluent Washington, D.C., suburb with a recent large influx of immigrants. The *Post* found that children from middle-class backgrounds in Montgomery County consistently scored very high on reading and math scores, even if they went to schools with a high concentration of poverty found in the student body.[10]

At Annandale High, our average SATs are often lower than in schools with homogeneous middle-income populations. But many of our students score high on the SATs and go on to the top universities in the country—Yale, Columbia, Duke, Northwestern, Johns Hopkins, William and Mary, University of Virginia—where they do exceptionally well. Plus, our students gained the broader world perspective that only a diverse institution can provide.

Some of the Annandale students with lower SAT scores were the first in their families to ever take an SAT test. Should the school's administration discourage them from taking the test so that the school's average looks better, as a real estate agent suggested to me? A truly good school wants every child to reach for the gold ring at every level, whether that means applying to Yale or being the first family member to sit for an

SAT exam. Annandale High encourages students to take the SAT multiple times, providing detailed guidance on how to improve the scores. If average scores are lower because more students take the test to learn from it, so be it.

The irony is that parents themselves are often the harshest critics of standardized tests. Whether attending a school chorus performance, a football game, or a PTA meeting, I hear parents decry the increasing emphasis on our statewide tests. A mother of an eighth grade student talks about the hives her daughter gets on the days she must take the new test that serves as a "gateway" to high school even if she passes every class. A father of a third grader laments the lack of teacher creativity he sees in the classrooms of his younger child. He says the same teacher was far more spirited and innovative when she taught his older child, before high-stakes standardized testing. Another mother worries that teachers must increasingly focus on the detailed facts that are on the tests, with little time left to cultivate the creativity or problem-solving skills she values.

And parent attitudes toward SAT tests are no better. Talk to the mother of a high school senior and you'll hear her complain that an SAT score can't adequately define her daughter, although it has the power to make or break her admission to the college of her dreams.

So if parents disparage the value of these tests, why do they believe that the average of student scores on these same tests are the one true measure of a school's value? Those of us who are connected with diverse schools know these tests tell only part of the story. Even if you believe that these tests do an adequate job measuring certain academic knowledge on a particular day, they do not capture the whole picture of academic growth.

Jamilah Alzer, a graduate of Annandale High in the late '90s, says she is much more aware of what is going on in the world because of the diverse population at her school. Annandale gave her the opportunity to "talk to people who came from places that you hear about in the news. I pay attention now to world events. I understand differences in countries and their media. When I hear a news report, I put that together with what my friends have said. I don't just accept what the news says."

Jamilah's advanced knowledge of the world quickly paid off when she began studying politics at college. "I'm more aware of different nationalities and cultures than students who didn't come from diverse schools. When we studied Ethiopia, many students had never heard of the border war with Eritrea. But I had two friends from Eritrea so I knew all about it."

Standardized tests do nothing to measure the crucial and intangible lessons that make our educational institutions so valuable to society. Melanie Pethcry, another Annandale graduate, sees the benefit of her diverse high school education as she studies to be a nurse. "All the students have to deal with patients from many different backgrounds. I don't have a problem dealing with anyone's culture or background. I can adjust much better than some of my classmates."

Standardized tests cannot measure integrity or openness to new ideas or tolerance, all lessons that are nurtured in a diverse environment. Annandale students know that test averages don't reflect what they can learn from the stunning art of a teen who spent his adolescence in a Kurdish refugee camp and eventually earned a $25,000 scholarship to study architecture at Pratt Institute, or from a girl who had left El Salvador only six months before choosing to sing "Climb Every Mountain" in the spring choral show.

You need to go beyond statistics to learn what a school is really like. You need to do some firsthand research. You need to talk to teachers and administrators about what is valued. You need to talk to parents whose kids are there today (not a mother whose son graduated in 1980 or a father whose daughter goes to a different school). You need to talk to students who can tell you what they learn from other students, in addition to their teachers. You need to attend football or basketball games, or watch a play or concert, and see how the students interact with each another. And most of all, you need to walk the halls in the school. You can't gain much insight from a page of statistics or a website.

At a meeting of parents of incoming ninth graders at the high school, I spoke with a mother whose son had attended a rigorous private academy through eighth grade. "People had warned me about the academic environment at Annandale High, talking about average SATs, so I explored for myself," she said. "I visited the high school. I sat in on classes. I talked to teachers. I was impressed." She went on to become an active parent at the high school, encouraging other neighbors with young children to dig beyond the test scores.

NOTES

1. Peter Sacks, "Predictable Losers in Testing Schemes," *School Administrator* 57, no. 11 (December 2000) 6–9.

2. Jean Johnson, "Will Parents and Teachers Get On the Bandwagon to Reduce School Size?" *Phi Delta Kappan* 83, no. 5 (January 2002): 353–56.

3. "WorkForce Technologies," Parent Satisfaction Survey Report, Fairfax County Public Schools, September 2001, 14.

4. For a discussion of Virginia parents' concerns with SOLs see, Mickey VanDerwerker and Roxanne Grossman, "The Truth about SOLs," Parents across Virginia United to Reform SOLs, 2000.

5. Daniel A. Domenech, "My Stakes Well Done," *School Administrator* 57, no. 11 (December 2000): 14–19.

6. W. James Popham, "Right Task, Wrong Tool," *American School Board Journal* 189, no. 2 (February 2002): 18–22.

7. For an excellent discussion of the value of integrating school populations economically, see Richard Kahlenberg's *All Together Now* (Washington, D.C.: Brookings Institution Press, 2001).

8. Alfie Kohn, *The Schools Our Children Deserve* (New York: Houghton Mifflin, 1999), 73.

9. Ellen Berg, "Teaching Students How to Give the Man What He Wants," *Middleweb, Exploring Middle School Reform*, 2002, www.middleweb.com/mw/msdiaries/01-02wklydiaries/EB18.html [accessed 15 June 2002].

10. Bridget Schultz and Dan Keating, "'Gifted' Grow Even in Weak Schools," *Washington Post*, 2 September 2001, 12A.

MYTH 2

One Style of School Leadership
Will Work in Every School

Many educators say, "I don't see color." You are doing yourself and others an extreme disservice by not seeing all around you the richness that should be celebrated, not ignored.

—Naeema Nuridden, "Cultural Diversity and the Schools"[1]

There is a special place in heaven for school principals. Their day begins before the sunrise. They take hundreds of kids under their wing each day. And their nights and weekends are usually filled with school meetings or events. All that for far less pay than their peers in law, medicine, or professional sports.

Many principals do a fantastic job as building leaders in the homogeneous white middle-class schools that were the norm in suburban America for several decades. But many neighborhoods are changing and so are the faces in the schools. The academic programs in some schools, however, have remained largely the same. After all, the well-meaning principal thinks, the school was working great, and "kids are kids." She watches in puzzlement, as teachers become frustrated, parents feel increasingly isolated, and students are less engaged in learning. The superintendent and school board meanwhile provide little support, arguing over who is to blame for problems in the school, secretly convinced it's the students who have become unteachable.

The prevailing myth would have us believe that the educational leaders are doing the best job they can because of their past record of student achievement. Since nothing else has changed, it has got to be the kids and their families. The reality, however, is that diverse schools need a new leadership paradigm.

Effective leadership of a diverse school begins with a state of mind. "First you've got to recognize the diversity within your student body and how that will affect students and their families," says Mary Barter, superintendent of schools in Durango, Colorado. Then you look at the "flip side of the coin," she says. "You've got to recognize that despite the diversity, the school is serving the same purpose for all those children and their families." Appreciating this commonality of purpose helps address issues of diversity when it becomes difficult, says Barter, an executive board member of the American Association for School Administrators with wide-ranging experience in urban, rural, and suburban schools.

A leader meets the challenge of building a successful diverse school by developing a positive school climate where students learn from each other in and out of the classroom. This type of environment doesn't happen by accident and it must be built from the top down. Joe Light, principal of Bowling Green Junior High School in Kentucky says that the overriding factor that has led to the success of his school is "the attitude that diversity is positive. We constantly preach the message that we learn from each other." And parents are listening.

"Diversity is drawing kids to our school," Light says. Bowling Green has students of many ethnic and racial backgrounds, some from families attracted by the strong economy of the area and others brought there by a nearby refugee center. Many are language-minority and from lower socioeconomic groups. Yet the school is so highly respected that about one-fourth of its students pay tuition to attend. Many of these students are from white middle-class families whose parents have moved out of the district, but don't want to leave the school. Others are children of faculty at nearby Western Kentucky University. "The parents believe that their children are going to be better educated if they are in a diverse environment than if they're not," Light says.

One of the key missions of an administrator in a diverse school must be to level the playing field—not to lower expectations, but to raise them for all and to reduce obstacles that prevent some children from achieving. Daniel Domenech, superintendent of Fairfax County Schools, took over the school system in 1998 as it was meeting new challenges of diversity, particularly in parts of the sprawling Virginia suburb that were closest to the urban center of Washington, D.C. Domenech himself immigrated to the United States from Cuba at age nine with little knowledge of English.

"You can't tailor one program to fit every student," says Domenech. "One that works with one student will fail with another. I've seen this mistake made over and over again. It creeps up on administrators," states Domenech. "They say, 'We're doing the same thing. It should work.' They don't understand why it won't work."

"If you believe as I do, that you have to meet the needs of every child, you quickly move in the direction of providing different programs for every child," Domenech says.

Under his leadership, Fairfax County, the twelfth largest school district in the nation, has adopted a number of innovative new programs. While Fairfax is known as a wealthy community, it also has large pockets of poverty that include an increasing number of recent immigrants from many cultures, particularly Asian, Latino, African, and Middle Eastern. Domenech has worked hard to convince the school board and the taxpayers that schools with more challenging demographics need extra resources. In a program that some considered to be a make-or-break effort for his term as superintendent, Domenech created "Project Excel" schools. The twenty lowest performing schools in the district are provided with extra resources, enabling them to provide extra services, such as full-day kindergarten, smaller class size, and more instructional time each week. These extra efforts are paying off in improved student achievement, particularly for the students in the early grades.

An educational leader must focus on leveling the playing field. This doesn't mean others lose out, just increased opportunities for all. At Rosemont Elementary School in Montgomery County, Maryland, school administrators partner with parent leaders to increase participation in the science fair, particularly by minority students. To begin on equal footing in a very visible way, the PTA provides every child with the three-sided display board and all topic headlines for the display. Clinics are held during lunch with volunteer parents and student teachers who help get students started on their projects, using resources in the technology lab and resource center. This could be assistance with picking topics, finding resource sites, and in some cases, helping the student begin the research. After school and during evening sessions, students who don't have a computer at home can type their projects and print out information and pictures for their displays.

The school has worked hard at engaging the parents. All flyers and resource information are translated into Spanish, the predominant minority language of the community. The school's staff parent liaison as well as volunteer parents, including bilingual parents, make phone calls and rally parent support. With the entire community working together, the school has seen a substantial schoolwide increase in participation in the science fair, including students of color. Each year school leaders look for new ways to improve outreach and help the increasingly diverse minority populations understand the value of a science fair and then find the resources to take part. Since populations of students from other cultures are increasing in the area, Rosemont may produce its materials in several languages in the future.

Leaders of well-run diverse schools are always on the lookout for new approaches to support their students. Instead of blaming parents for not connecting with schools in the traditional way, an effective leader analyzes the obstacles to their participation and creates new ways for them to connect. Susan Akroyd, principal at Parklawn Elementary School in Fairfax County, a school with almost 800 students from some 34 countries, recognizes that parent involvement is directly related to student success. Among the school's many outreach strategies is hiring a bus to pick up parents at apartment buildings for important meetings. At the school meetings, the parents find interpreters and babysitters.

Akroyd has also built a novel support system for families in the community. Her school uses federal Title I schoolwide funds to create a family education center in an apartment in the heart of her community. The parents can come to the Parklawn Family Center during the day or evening for parenting classes, English classes, or simple opportunities to support the school such as cutting pictures from magazines for arts and crafts projects. The center provides lots of opportunities for parents to learn alongside their children, whether through interactive programs for preschoolers and their parents or special literacy programs for school-age children. School officials are frequent visitors to the center, helping the parents learn more about the curriculum and how to assist their children. The result of all the efforts? In a school where traditional approaches to parent outreach would fall flat, Parklawn has seen an increase in attendance at parent-teacher conferences and schoolwide events. And equally important, many of Parklawn's minority parents are better equipped to work with their students at home. Akroyd says:

> We need to carefully consider what we mean by parent involvement because the definition in the old paradigm—parent involvement is only volunteering in the school—is obsolete. Classroom volunteer work is just one of many ways in which parents and families are involved in the life of their children. The mere fact that a parent reads to a child or talks on the phone to a staff member or talks to other parents about their children's learning is parent involvement.

The leaders of today's successful diverse schools are ingenious and dogged as they use every contact they can think of to build on the resources of the school. Superintendent Vic Meyers of Colorado Springs, Colorado, says, "We seek out community groups to partner with—the Black Chamber of Commerce, the Asian Chamber of Commerce, the Hispanic Chamber of Commerce, and the NAACP. We try to keep the community informed and to build as many partnerships as possible." One example of that creative approach is a collaboration with the Community Partnership for Child Development, which provides Head Start and other preschool opportunities at every one of the elementary schools in Meyers's district, with funding from state education and special education funds.

That same collaborative effort is at work in Rockland County, New York, building a sense of community beyond the school walls. Over half the schools in Rockland County have a Family Resource Center, tailored to meet the needs of that individual community. Parents from that neighborhood, including parents from different races and ethnic groups, come together to make their school more family friendly. They identify the needs of their community and then determine what the school can provide to meet those needs. The center offers wide-ranging services from early education and after-school programs, to parent support, health and medical services, and information and referral for additional services. "This is a place where families of all different backgrounds can really work together," says Mimi Hoffman of the Rockland 21st-Century Collaboration for Children and Youth.

Principal Jo Anne Hughes of Dallas' Walnut Hill Elementary has built a remarkable support network for the students at her diverse school. "I'm always asking for help: anyone, everyone," she says. The school has an active business partnership with IBM, which includes an "e-mentor" over the Internet with every student in third through sixth grade. Additional mentors and tutors visit the school from Raytheon Corporation, the Golden Kiwanis (senior members of Kiwanis), and a private high school nearby.

Hughes is always looking for ways to involve more parents. Walnut Hill not only has an active traditional PTA, the school is also supported by a fathers' group called the "Do-Dads." "These fathers found an important niche for themselves. Plus they provide an emotional boost to the staff," says Hughes, noting the faculty provides a weekly list of projects for them. In addition to doing "leg work and back work," the fathers provide a weekly one-minute announcement for the entire school. It began when there was some political upheaval in the school system and one of the fathers made an announcement to say how much he appreciated the dedication of the Walnut Hill faculty. Hughes found it so valuable, she invited the group to make a weekly announcement.

The fathers' messages range from poems they've read or written to quotes and stories or personal insights. Royce Smith wrote an anagram using all the letters of Walnut Hill. He began, "W is for workers. You have to work hard to be a winner and we know you are winners by having won the National Blue Ribbon Award. We are proud you are hard workers." For U, he told the students at Walnut Hill, where nearly one quarter of the students are identified as having special needs, they are unique. "All the way from pre-K to sixth grade and our special needs students, each one is unique. Our special needs students are so special to us and are so important to making Walnut Hill a well-rounded school Yes, we are proud of you." He ended by putting the last two L's together for "life-long learners. None of us stop learning when the school bell rings. The adults are still learning from you."

To make a diverse environment a healthy learning environment, leaders must view differences in beliefs and practices not as a burden to be overcome, but as human qualities to be respected and learned from. The school administration can find many ways to meet the needs of individuals without infringing on the rights of others. And all the students learn valuable lessons. During Ramadan when Muslims fast during daylight, Annandale High offers Muslim students a classroom where they can study during lunch so they don't have to enter the cafeteria. Because Ramadan is an accepted part of the school culture, just about every student is knowledgeable about the holiday. At a girls' basketball game, a parent mentioned to her daughter that the star player wasn't doing well that night. "Come on, Mom," her daughter replied, "Don't you know that it's Ramadan and she's been fasting all day!" While too many people in our society have only stereotypes to associate with Muslims, Annandale High students think of basketball players who fast from sunup to sundown and still go out on the court at night to support the school.

Diverse schools can be exciting places that benefit all the students, the faculty, and the community. But leaders can't follow the handbook from 1960 and expect a multiethnic school to function as it should. This style of leadership may meet the needs of some students, but it certainly won't meet the needs of the community or our society at large. At worst, the school may become a hotbed of tension between ethnic or racial groups feeling underserved by an inattentive or even biased administration. It's far better to be proactive than wait for a damaging outburst to serve as a wake-up call, requiring months or even years of repair before a positive, healthy school environment can be forged.

The challenge for school leadership is to face the obstacles early, tackle them with energy and creativity, and build a school on a foundation of respect and high expectations where everyone reaps the benefits. The toughest part is that this is a continuing challenge, because what works today won't work the same next year or the year after.

NOTE

1. Naeema Nuridden, "Cultural Diversity and the Schools," *Equity News* (Winter 1999).

MYTH 3

The Best Teachers Prefer
Homogeneous Middle-Class Schools

> When we as educators allow our pedagogy to be radically changed
> by our recognition of a multi-cultural world, we can give our stu-
> dents the education they desire and deserve.
>
> —bell hooks, *Teaching to Transgress:*
> *Education as the Practice of Freedom*[1]

No doubt about it, teaching is one tough profession. I've watched my husband devote his mind and soul to the children he taught, rarely having a night or weekend when he didn't do schoolwork. And then I listened to my daughter as she followed in her father's footsteps, not only bringing home hours of work but also the stories of kids' achievements, frustrations, and personal obstacles over which she had no control. Many of our friends are teachers, and at one point I had to enforce a time limit on "teacher talk" during social get-togethers because these folks live and breathe their work.

This isn't a job to those who dedicate their lives to it. It's truly a calling. If you were meant to be a teacher, you have to be in that classroom. Unfortunately, fewer are answering that calling. While we say that our society values teachers, we actually push bright creative young people away from the classroom. A high-achieving young woman will be advised to look beyond teaching, reminded that her options aren't limited as they were a generation ago. She can take her pick of jobs that pay more and enable her to have a more sophisticated lifestyle. (Ask a teacher when she last went out for lunch.) If you are a young man at the top of your college class, try telling your father that you've opted to teach third grade instead of going to law school.

While most adults can readily tell you the name of a teacher who made a difference in their lives, many will advise their children against majoring in education. My daughter expressed frustration at the well-meaning family friends (many teachers themselves) who suggested she could be so much more than a teacher, yet that is all she wanted to be her whole life.

But some of the brightest, most thoughtful, and creative young people are still choosing to teach. And they are after the gold ring of teaching—touching children's lives. And there are also an increasing number of teachers who have answered the calling in their second careers. First they were lawyers or accountants or engineers like others told them they were supposed to be. And then at some point, they realized they needed more. Not more money, not more prestige. They needed to make more of a difference.

For many, the meaning they seek becomes crystal clear at a diverse school. They love the challenge of reaching so many different types of students and providing just what they need to excel. They love the richness of resources in their own classroom and the community—not resources of paper and computer disks, but of human souls with life experiences that teach many lessons. And they love the appreciation of students who have overcome grave adversity to be sitting in that classroom, students who truly understand the value of free education.

"The diversity of Annandale High is *the* reason I applied here," says veteran English teacher Virginia Crowley. With a husband in the military, Crowley has taught in different ends of the United States, from Florida to New Mexico to Ohio, as well as in Turkey and Germany. "Working with students from so many backgrounds, I knew what a rich blend a diverse student body makes. It is energizing to me to have students who are not all clones of one another," says Crowley who has turned down offers from other schools closer to her home.

Math teacher Donna Erickson also specifically sought a job at Annandale High because of its mix of students, and left a predominantly white school to be part of the Annandale staff. "The diversity empowers the whole classroom because the students have so many different backgrounds and experiences from which all can benefit."

Tom Pratuch, a National Board Certified chemistry teacher, came to teaching late in life after a stint with the Army, working for the Catholic Church, and a career in computers. He got his master's in education and substitute taught at a lot of schools, finding out what he liked and didn't like in a school environment. Annandale High was at the top of his list and he was thrilled that he was on the top of theirs as well.

Pratuch is outspoken on the myth of diverse schools not attracting quality teachers. He distinguishes between "good" teachers and "the best" teachers. "It's really hard to differentiate your instruction," which is necessary in a diverse classroom, he says. Most teachers are trained to reach a uniform population and that's what they are comfortable with, Pratuch says. "So, many good teachers seek out homogeneous schools."

But if you are talking about "the best" teachers, Pratuch says you should look no further than diverse schools. "I think you get a disproportionately higher number of the best teachers at truly diverse schools—schools that are diverse in races, ethnic groups, economic background, and abilities. Just look at who is winning the national awards and major grants. They are predominantly from diverse schools," he says.

"What's in my heart, and what I hear from others, is that if you really want to have a positive effect on kids, you are drawn to diverse schools. Why go somewhere the kids don't need you?"

Good teachers are drawn to challenging schools where the leadership respects their professional competence, like Walnut Hill Elementary School in Dallas. "We have the talent we need here to solve any academic problem, we just need to break through the system," says principal Jo Anne Hughes, who was the 1988–1989 Dallas Principal of the Year. "Schools are set up to isolate teachers," Hughes says. "We find ways to break down the barriers and let them work together to meet the needs of our students." Walnut Hill has had four teachers among the finalists for Dallas Teacher of the Year and one teacher recognized as a Disney American Teacher.

Many teachers in diverse schools talk about the daily lessons they learn from their students. Teachers at Woodrow Wilson Elementary School in Binghamton, New York, have a saying, "The teachers are the 'tall' teachers and the students are the 'small' teachers," says Kate Andreatta, who is a representative of National Education Association in New York. In her upstate New York community with immigrants from countries like the Ukraine, Russia, Vietnam, Africa, Haiti, and Bosnia, the teachers recognize that "all of us collectively learn more than each of us does individually," she says.

"The world really is a small place and all of us come with similarities and differences," says Andreatta. "In fact, we're more alike than we are different. When you put all of us together, we learn so much."

Teachers often tell you they are touched on a daily basis by students whose families have come to the United States seeking opportunity, particularly a first-rate education. These students are motivated to achieve, but face many obstacles, including parents who are not skilled at helping them through the American school system.

Erin Albright, the coordinator of the International Baccalaureate program at Annandale High, talks about meeting with a young man who had left South America with his family a few years earlier, just a year shy of graduating from high school there. With the burden of learning a new language, he had been placed in his sophomore year again in the United States, and had battled to get to his senior year. He was committed to succeeding, but was struggling with an advanced English class.

Albright called him in to her office and told him she wanted to meet with him on a daily basis to keep track of his progress and see how she could help. Seeing his eyes tear up, she assured him this wasn't for punishment, but for support. "I understand," he said in his new language. "I'm just so happy someone will take care of me." Her eyes teared up as well.

Certainly there are caring, competent teachers who are drawn to schools with homogeneous middle-class populations. The truth is, different teachers work better in different teaching environments. Every child deserves a teacher who wakes up in the morning and wants to be there. I watched a gifted and creative music teacher become totally ineffective when she was moved from a middle-class white school to one with a range in ethnicity and socioeconomic status. But similarly, many exceptional teachers find their heart is in a diverse school.

Principal Ben Bushman from Beverly Hills High School, with students from fifty-six countries, says he has no problem finding competent teachers. "The myth of diverse schools not attracting good teachers is just that, a myth. More often than not, I see good teachers asking to be in a diverse environment," he says.

Annandale High principal, Donald Clausen, agrees. "It's becoming easier and easier to find good staff. Teachers are seeking us out."

Grace Taylor, principal of Atlanta's Cross Keys Elementary School, the most culturally diverse in the state of Georgia, calls her staff "incredible." "So many teachers go above and beyond. They are always doing plays or holding discussions or organizing hands-on projects or debates," she says.

There is no question that teaching in a diverse school can be extremely challenging, but many teachers enter the field because they love the challenge. Roni Silverstein, assistant principal in Rosemont Elementary School in Gaithersburg, Maryland, says that the teachers at diverse schools are often on the cutting edge of their profession. "Because leaders of diverse schools constantly have to pedal hard to reach all our kids, when we hire we look for the best and the brightest teachers. Many of our staff are young and enthusiastic teachers who have been trained in new 'best practices,'" she says.

"When we interview new teachers, we lay on the table that this is not an easy job. But I've had no problem attracting teachers," Silverstein says. "It really is a calling."

Don't fall prey to myths about the quality of teaching in a diverse school. Sit in a classroom and hear firsthand the commitment these teachers have. When you talk to teachers in a well-run diverse school, you'll hear passionate stories from educators who believe that it is the diversity itself that makes it an exciting and fulfilling place to teach.

NOTE

1. bell hooks, *Teaching to Transgress: Education as the Practice of Freedom* (New York: Rouledge, 1994).

4

MYTH 4

Diverse Schools Can't Provide Rigorous Classes

Students learn more and think in deeper, more complex ways in a diverse educational environment. . . . For an educational institution, the challenge obviously is to find ways to engage the deeper, less automatic mode of thinking. Complex thinking occurs when people encounter a novel situation for which, by definition, they have no script, or when the environment demands more than their current scripts provide.

—Patricia Gurin, "The Compelling Need for Diversity in Higher Education"[1]

Many parents assume—they don't investigate—that diverse schools don't offer academic challenges to their students. However, a core element of a successful diverse school is the belief that every child, of every background, can and should succeed at a high level. Educational leaders committed to that ideal offer challenging academic programs, encourage students to reach for new heights, and identify ways to support those who are struggling to meet the challenge. They often offer innovative opportunities for all students that could only be possible with a diverse student body.

"We take every child from where they are academically when they come into the school and lead them to where they should be," says Jeri

Kitner a teacher at Walnut Hill Elementary School in Dallas. A school with a population of Hispanic, African American, and Caucasian students, 50 percent qualifying for free or reduced lunch, Walnut Hill has built a successful school on its foundation of high standards for all. In 1999, the U.S. Department of Education named it a Blue Ribbon School.

Walnut Hill offers a variety of options for its younger students that have attracted many students from other Dallas schools. "There are no cookie cutter molds at our school," Kitner says. Parents can choose traditional kindergarten, first, and second grade classes; or mixed-aged classes of K–1, 1–2, and 2–3. Kindergarten teachers move up to first grade with their students and loop back down to kindergarten, a strategy that builds on the developing bond between student and teacher.

Another option takes advantage of the strengths of Walnut Hill's mixed population. The school offers dual immersion classrooms for kindergarten and first grade, comprised of half English speakers and half Spanish speakers. As this group of students progresses, the school is adding a dual immersion class in each grade through six grade. "As they study together, these students will be fluent in both languages," Kitner says.

A commitment to a high level of achievement for every student led Annandale High School Principal Donald Clausen to create an Academic Task Force. A collaborative body of administrators, teachers, parents, and community members, the task force meets regularly to review the academic programs in the school to help ensure that the needs of all the students are being met. One of the first recommendations of the task force was to bring in a prestigious new program for top achievers, the International Baccalaureate (IB). The task force believed this would add opportunities that the current offerings of Advanced Placement courses could not provide.

In most locations, the IB program is run largely as a school within a school, limited to only those students who are able to follow the demanding requirements that lead to an IB Diploma. But at Annandale, school leadership is committed to bringing the advantages of IB to as many students as possible. Annandale's program not only offers the opportunity to pursue the full IB Diploma, but it encourages any motivated student to take one or more IB classes in the subjects in which they excel and go after a certificate in that class. There is a commitment to identifying capable students for these classes who may not identify themselves. "We work to remove obstacles for students and parents to access advanced services," says Annandale's IB coordinator, Erin Albright. "We worry less about getting someone into the program who doesn't belong and more about leaving someone out who does belong."

In an attempt to bring academic challenge to a broader mix of capable students, Annandale High offers several IB classes that can be taken by students who are learning English as a new language. Many of these new English speakers already speak several languages but they don't have the advanced fluency in English to take challenging American high school classes (a process that can take seven years[2]). Annandale High offers a Spanish class for near-fluent speakers, which has attracted a broad mix of students from native Spanish speakers who seek the opportunity to study Spanish literature and culture in an academic setting, to those born in the United States who have lived in Spanish-speaking countries, to graduates of a Spanish immersion program offered at one of the elementary schools. Every student brings a particular strength to the class which benefits the whole class. The school also offers an IB English class for near-fluent speakers, providing a strong academic approach to English language and literature for those who haven't attained full fluency.

The rigorous IB offerings at Annandale don't ignore the arts, with IB classes in subjects such as music theory and drama. The IB art class has been "absolutely stupendous," says teacher Joyce Weinstein, an accomplished artist herself whose work has been shown internationally. The students must develop a project with their own theme to fulfill their IB requirements. Many of them use their own cultures as a foundation, says Weinstein.

One Vietnamese girl used Vietnamese folk tales as the basis for her entire body of work. "She researched and wrote about the tales, and took a museum trip searching for imagery and information about them," Weinstein says. Another student who was born in Columbia researched imagery from pre-Columbian art, which became her theme. A boy who had lived in the Sudan and Yemen chose to work on the theme of human suffering, based on what he had seen. His paintings are "quite amazing," says Weinstein. "They transcend the cartoon and grotesque and become universal themes," she says.

"This is the best work that has ever come out of my classroom," said the veteran teacher. The students in Weinstein's IB art class all learned a tremendous amount from each other's work in addition to developing their own talents. Since part of the IB assessment is to have the students talk about their work, the students questioned each other after the project was done, gaining insight into the different histories and cultures.

Many leaders of diverse schools pride themselves on the wide range of programs they institute, increasing opportunities for students to succeed. In addition to the IB program, Annandale offers a variety of initiatives. In its active College Partnership, a collaborative program with nearly thirty colleges along with business and industry, Annandale guidance counselors and teachers work with promising students of color and their parents from the day they enter the school to help the students successfully enroll and achieve in college. Advancement Via Individual Determination (AVID) is an intensive classroom-based approach that encourages successful minority students who were not on a college track to pursue postsecondary education. Recognizing that many students need assistance in the transition to high school, Annandale works with the middle schools in an intensive four-year support program that focuses on at-risk students prior to ninth grade and works with them year round.

Beverly Hills High School, unlike the TV portrayal of the high school in its zip code, is a very diverse mix of students from fifty-six countries. One-third of the student body was born outside the United States. "In the lunch room, I look around and see kids from Trinidad, Iran, Turkey, Israel, Japan, Korea," says Principal Ben Bushman.

Beverly Hills is known for its strong academic program. The school takes the strengths of a large school—resources and opportunities—and combines them with the personal attention of a smaller school. Students are grouped into three mixed-grade houses of about 700 students, each with a vice principal, three counselors, and staff.

Bushman is proud of the school's recognition by the U.S. Department of Education as a National Blue Ribbon School. "Minorities are represented in all our rigorous programs," Bushman states. "There is an expectation of high achievement through the entire school system." Foreign languages, algebra, and sometimes geometry start in middle school.

There is a large Advanced Placement program, beginning in the sopho-more year, with students scoring far above the national average on the rigorous national tests.

One of the strengths of Beverly Hills is in the broad-based electives offered to the students. "There is something for everyone," says Bush-man, citing the performing arts band, orchestra, forty-six different ath-letic teams, weekly newspaper, and the longest-running school-based TV news show in the country.

Diverse schools can and do provide academic challenge for their stu-dents. In well-run diverse schools all over the country, this challenge goes hand in hand with a belief that every child is capable of meeting high expectations. The added attraction in these schools is that their dis-tinctive population mix can provide enhanced academic opportunities for every student that are not possible with homogeneous populations.

NOTES

1. Patricia Gurin, "The Compelling Need for Diversity in Higher Educa-tion," Expert testimony in *Gratz et al. v. Bollinger et al.* (No. 97-75231 E.D. Mich., filed 1997; and No. 97-75972 E.D. Mich., filed 1997), 1999.

2. Virginia Collier, "Age and Rate of Acquisition of Second Language for Academic Purposes," *TESOL Quarterly* 21, no. 4 (1987): 617–41.

MYTH 5

Diverse Schools Are Not Safe

How are we ever going to get where we need to be in this county if we're afraid to put our kids in school where they are going to meet other kinds of people?

—Ayobamidele Odejimi, student at Annandale High School

I was having dinner with friends from out of town, talking about the academic enrichment of diverse schools, as I often do. They both nodded their heads in agreement, as I bubbled over with my enthusiasm. I'm never really sure what people think in those situations, since I probably don't give them much room to disagree.

A few days later, I got an e-mail from one of them. "Our conversation got me thinking about diversity. I know that I heartily like the idea of diversity and would fully support it except for one thing—the fear factor. The fear of my kids or myself being in a dangerous school environment is really what keeps me from thinking more positively about the issue."

She nailed on the head one of the major concerns of parents, all parents: that their child's school be safe and secure. And she gave voice to the myth that controls many parents' thinking: diverse schools just aren't safe.

Safety is clearly an issue in some schools. In many cases, the safety concerns reflect the troubled environment of the surrounding community, often one minority group locked in a pocket of poverty. It is a difficult burden for teachers, parents, and students. Yet there are dedicated school leaders who do rise above these burdens and create a safe school environment.

That being said, however, it is a great leap, and an invalid one, for parents to assume that any school with a mix of students that includes racial and ethnic minorities will be unsafe. We've seen the most horrific kind of school violence—a small group of students who opened fire on their fellow students and teachers—happen in a largely middle-class school that was more than 90 percent Caucasian. In fact, many of school shootings in recent years have been in schools that are predominantly white.[1]

A "diverse" school as defined throughout this book, has students from a broad range of races and ethnicities and, in the ideal, from different socioeconomic groups. It is critical to avoid knee-jerk reactions to changing school populations and investigate to uncover the facts. Many schools with multiethnic and multiracial populations have excellent records on safety, many with less gang activity and fewer incidents of violence than largely white schools.

The mix of students in a diverse school actually spurs the leadership to take bold steps to build a positive school climate, because effective leaders of diverse schools know they can't run on automatic pilot. They know that they must have their eyes open at all times and be proactive. Annandale High School doesn't have metal detectors or video cameras; instead it has caring and attentive adult eyes watching over the student body.

"Students in diverse schools need more individual attention, so our administrators and guidance staff are very tuned into what is happening with our students," says Annandale High Principal Donald Clausen. This proactive stance, rather than a reaction to individual acts of violence, is essential to creating a safe school environment, according to the Public Education Network, a national association of community-based organizations advancing school reform.[2]

I am always amazed at the way Annandale administrators seem to know not only what is going on at that moment, but where to focus attention in the future. I remember the senior class photo one year, a large mass of more than 500 students where each head was a small dot on the wide page. Principal Clausen examined it shortly after it was taken and noticed that one student was holding his hands in a way that could be viewed as a gang sign. Clausen took immediate action. The picture was airbrushed and the offending student paid for the change. His parents were notified. I can't help but contrast that with a principal in a now in-famous white middle-class high school who didn't even know there was a group of troubled students who wore their trench coats in school every day to identify themselves.

"You can make assumptions in middle-class white schools that every-one is fine and everything is OK," says Clausen. "But sooner or later ad-ministrators find out that everything isn't as wonderful as it appears. We're very aggressive about knowing what is going on and we can stay on top of things."

The belief that the administrators in strong diverse schools are par-ticularly diligent was echoed by Carolyn Tabarini. Tabarini is in a unique place to know what's happening in her school—she was elected PTA president at Groveton Elementary and later was hired as the secretary to the school principal. "This is definitely a place where all the children feel safe," says Tabarini of her school in Fairfax County, Virginia, where students hail from nearly thirty countries. "The administrators deal with things as they happen. I've seen so many situations that were handled immediately; situations that could have escalated if not dealt with." Again, this contrasts with stories I hear all the time of small problems ig-nored in predominantly white schools. Sooner or later, they become big problems.

It's not just the administrators who are on top of things. At well-run diverse schools, everyone—faculty, support staff, students—look out for one another. Many diverse schools have active peer mediation pro-grams, where students are trained to help classmates deal with small dis-agreements before they become full-blown problems. In Chula Vista School District, a large kindergarten through sixth grade district at the southern tip of California, student mediators are called the "Peace Pa-trol." Selected by teachers, the members are trained to listen and assist in problem-solving conflicts and disagreements among students, partic-ularly on the playground. They wear specially designed jackets to help identify them.

The peer mediators at Annandale High School have received national recognition, testifying before Congress and facilitating workshops at the

National Mediation Conference at George Mason University. "As soon as we get students together and we start asking open-ended questions, giving each person time to talk, they listen to each other," says student mediator Danni Rumber. "They realize how small or even petty the problem was. When you are angry, you can't always see that."

"The myth that diverse schools are unsafe baffles me," says Rumber. "I've never felt unsafe here, never threatened, never felt something might happen to me."

In a well-run diverse school, students mix across races and cultures in classes and after school. That social integration among races and cultures was found to be a major factor in "school connectedness"—a student's feeling of being part of and cared for at school—in the National Longitudinal Study of Adolescent Health. This critical connection to school has been identified as a powerful protective factor against a number of risky behaviors among teenagers.[3] Justin, a junior at Logan High in Union City, California, says that there is always someone you can feel comfortable with at his school, which has a student body composed of many different races and cultures. "I'm Filipino and I've made friends with people of other cultures. There is no one with no friends because there is always someone to relate to. You never see anyone alone," he says.

Many parents are living under the misguided assumption that minority students are the root of violent behavior in schools. The 2001 Surgeon General's report on youth violence reviewed a massive body of research, including confidential surveys in which students reported the serious violent acts they have committed. The report concludes that one of the major "myths about youth violence" is that "African American and Hispanic youths are more likely to become involved in violence than other racial or ethnic groups." Calling these myths "intrinsically dangerous," the report states, "Myths may trigger public fears and lead to inappropriate or misguided policies that result in inefficient or counterproductive use of scarce public resources."[4]

The unfounded belief that schools with many recent immigrants are unsafe can be easily debunked by talking to parents whose children attend diverse schools. It's obvious to many of us that recent immigrants are often stricter parents, giving their students far less freedom to misbehave than many middle-class American-born parents.

I remember listening to a panel of parents from different ethnic backgrounds speak at a high school parent meeting. The Middle Eastern mother noted that one of the American customs that puzzles her is sleep-overs. "It is very difficult for me to let my daughter spend the night in the home of someone who is not a relative. I do not even know the family beyond saying 'hello.'"

The Hispanic mother relayed that most social events in their culture involve the family, not the child—even a teenager—going out alone. My white friend whispered in my ear, "Now I understand why Marta's entire family came to my daughter's birthday party with her last year!" I couldn't help envying the other cultures' strong family bonds, recognizing that the vast majority of American teenagers would be mortified to spend their Saturday nights with their parents.

Research supports the view that recent immigrants are strong parents. Studies show that first-generation immigrant youth—those born outside the United States—are less involved in risky behaviors than students whose families have lived in this country for a generation or two. For the most part, these rates are lower than that of the white population.[5]

Many middle class parents believe that their children will be protected from gangs if they remain locked in their segregated suburbs, avoiding schools with minority students. Again, the facts reveal otherwise. Documenting the growth in gangs in recent decades, the U.S. Department of Justice reported "a striking increase in the growth of gang problems in the Nation's smaller cities, towns, and villages."[6] I heard Fairfax County police officials shock parents by letting them know that the biggest growth of gangs in our sprawling county is in the affluent western region. There have been far more recent incidences of serious gang violence in predominantly white schools than in the diverse schools of our county. On their website, the county police make it clear that gangs are not someone else's problem. "Q. Where are gangs found? A. Everywhere. . . . Gangs develop in areas where they are not bothered—where no one pays attention to them such as shopping malls, playgrounds, parks, and the house next door."

Tim Wise, a national antibias activist, chastises his fellow whites for ignoring the violence in white schools, writing, "White people live in an utter state of self-delusion. We think danger is black, brown, and poor, and if we can just move far enough away from 'those people' in the cities we'll be safe. If we can just find an 'all-American' town, life will be better, because things like this just don't happen here.'"[7]

Wise went on to directly address the issues of alcohol and drug use by youth, a major factor in school safety, citing well-respected government statistics. "According to the Centers for Disease Control and Prevention and the U.S. Department of Health and Human Services, it is your children and not those of the urban ghetto who are most likely to use drugs," he wrote to his white peers.

> That's right: white high school students are seven times more likely than blacks to have used cocaine; eight times more likely to have smoked crack; ten times more likely to have used LSD; seven times more likely to have used heroin. In fact, there are more white high school students who have used crystal methamphetamine (the most addictive drug on the streets) than there are black students who smoke cigarettes.
>
> What's more, white youth ages 12–17 are more likely to sell drugs: 34 percent more likely, in fact than their black counterparts. And it is white youth who are twice as likely to binge drink, and nearly twice as likely than blacks to drive drunk. And white males are twice as likely to bring a weapon to school as are black males.[8]

Former Annandale High Principal Ray Watkins used to enjoy giving his principal colleagues a pop quiz. He would ask them to name the schools with the fewest incidents of physical violence out of the twenty-three high schools in our system. None would guess correctly that Annandale High had a lower record of violence than most of the predominantly white high schools. When I spoke to the Annandale Rotary Club in the mid '90s, a group basically of older white men, I asked them which school had reported a student with a weapon in school that year. None would remember that it had been an affluent white school, even though there were major headlines when it occurred a month earlier. However, they all remembered the negative headlines about Annandale High from several years earlier, when fights were reported as the school population rapidly changed. The negative headlines about Annandale simply confirm their misconception that diverse schools are not safe, so they retain them far longer than the news reports about violence at a middle-class white school where it "just doesn't happen."

It's time to open our eyes to the reality. Youth violence is a problem and it needs to be addressed. But, as the surgeon general advises, believing in myths about school safety is counterproductive and dangerous. Don't make assumptions based on demographic data. If you want to find out if a school is safe, investigate. Walk the halls. Talk to parents. Talk to students. Talk to teachers. Talk to the principal. You may find that a diverse school is the place your child feels safest.

NOTES

1. "A Time Line of Recent School Shootings," *Infoplease.com*, *Learning Network*. infoplease.com/ipa/A0777958.html [accessed 15 June 2002]; demographic data from National Center for Educational Statistics, www.nces.ed.gov/nceskids/index.html [accessed 15 June 2002].

2. Public Education Network, *Increasing Safety in America's Public Schools: Lessons from the Field* (Washington, D.C.: Author, 2001), 6.

3. R. W. Blum and C. A. McNeely, *Improving the Odds: The Untapped Power of Schools to Improve the Health of Teens*, Center for Adolescent Health and Development, University of Minnesota (Minneapolis: University of Minnesota, 2000).

4. *Youth Violence: A Report of the Surgeon General* (Washington, D.C.: U.S. Department of Health and Human Services, 2001), Executive Summary, 4–5.

5. Kathleen Mullan Harris, "Health Risk Behavior among Adolescents in Immigrant Families," Population Center, University of North Carolina at Chapel Hill. Paper presented at the Urban Seminar Series on Children's Health and Safety, December 2–3, 1999, at Harvard University.

6. Walter B. Miller, *The Growth of Youth Gang Problems in the United States: 1970–98*, (Washington, D.C.: Office of Juvenile Justice and Delinquency Prevention, U.S. Department of Justice, 2001), x.

7. Tim Wise, "School Shootings and White Denial," *AlterNet.org*, www.alternet.org/story.html?StoryID=10560, 6 March 2001 [accessed 15 June 2002].

8. Tim Wise, "School Shootings."

MYTH 6

Family Beliefs and Values Will Be Threatened If We Expose Our Youth to People with Different Perspectives

Preservation of one's own culture does not require contempt or disrespect for other cultures.

—Cesar Chavez[1]

One day in November during my daughter's freshman year at Annandale High, she got off the bus and immediately got on the phone with a friend she had left a few minutes earlier. She came into the kitchen an hour later, recounting with teenage enthusiasm the lengthy dialogue she had on the bus and afterward with her new friend Susie. Sara hadn't encountered anyone with Susie's perspective on life before. Susie regularly attends a fundamentalist Christian church with her family. Sara, on the other hand, had an extensive Jewish education and was active in her family's synagogue.

This day Susie and Sara were discussing the role of women in the family and society. Next week, they'd be talking about gays in the military (a policy in the news at the time). A month later, they'd tackle affirmative action.

Did Susie and Sara come to consensus on issues? Rarely. Did they change each other's thinking? Occasionally. Did they enjoy the intellectual challenge? You bet. Did they respect each other? Absolutely. In fact, they became close friends that year and remain so ten years later. "I've always appreciated a relationship where we could mutually challenge each other," says Susie Gaskins, "and Sara sure did that."

Actually, Sara's group of high school friends remain largely intact several years beyond college. In another community the makeup of the group might cause eyebrows to be raised: Christian, Jewish, Sikh, Buddhist, Catholic; parents from Thailand, the Philippines, Vietnam, India, and Korea. These young adults have maintained their own identities, both religiously and culturally, but seek out interchange with people of other backgrounds.

Sara's friend Jaspreet Singh identifies strongly with his Indian heritage, organizing a large international conference for Indian students at college, but he also treasures his contacts beyond his group. "If I am Indian and I meet another Indian, we share a culture. But having Filipino and Vietnamese and Jewish friends, we still share an experience. We all have different backgrounds thrown into the mix, and there is a benefit to that."

What I have seen over and over is that young people do not have to be surrounded by those who share their beliefs at all times to feel those beliefs have merit. Yes, it is important that children learn the values and culture of their family. But in most cases, these beliefs are strengthened by exposure to other students from different backgrounds.

Parent Jaime Bacigalupi sent three children to Annandale High School after they attended the nearby Catholic school through eighth grade. She was one of a number of parents who wanted a more intense religious education for their children at earlier grades and then sought the benefits of the public schools when the children were older. According to Bacigalupi, her children's values were never threatened by attending a diverse high school. "If anything their values have been strengthened and have grown by the sheer exposure to a broader base," she says. "If you only live within the boundaries of your values, then you have no idea of the strength of those values. If they are never challenged, never questioned, never tested, you don't grow."

Annandale High parent Andrea Sobel has been impressed that her daughter Gina has friends in most of her classes from different cultures, yet is strengthened in her own identity with Judaism. "I find this significant as it emphasizes the multicultural nature of our community, rather than the 'melting pot' point of view, encouraging students to be comfortable in expressing their individuality in beliefs and culture."

Students of many backgrounds feel the school environment motivates them to dig deeper into their own heritage. "Being part of a diverse school made me respect other cultures," says Melanie Pethcry, an Annandale High graduate whose mother is Thai and father Filipino. "But it made me want to share who I am, too."

Annandale graduate Alex Berens was raised in the Jewish religion of his father but also shares the Vietnamese culture of his mother. Berens vividly remembers class discussions at Annandale where people from different parts of the world contributed unique perspectives, making the discussions engaging and thought provoking. "You didn't want to misrepresent where you are from or how you were raised, so it encouraged a lot of study about who you are."

The kids at Annandale often discuss religion and race, topics that many adults find difficult to trod. My daughter, Sara, regularly wore her Star of David, a symbol of Judaism, to school as a way to identify herself and open discussion. That also led her to strengthen her own understanding of her heritage. "I felt a responsibility to know what I was talking about, so I often researched the Jewish perspective on issues, talking to my parents and our rabbi."

Jamilah Alzer says she felt completely comfortable expressing her Muslim beliefs at Annandale. "All my friends would understand because they had their own religion—Christian, Hindi, Buddhist, Jewish. When I would talk about fasting during Ramadan, someone would talk about fasting on Yom Kippur or not eating meat on Fridays." Students would ask why she didn't cover her head, inspiring her to clarify her thoughts about the custom.

Ayobamidele Odejimi says that he and his friends at Annandale High bring religion into discussions on many issues. He and my son, Alex, frequently discussed the Jewish versus Baptist view of issues. It didn't change his values, he says, it just informs his view of the world.

"People ask; people talk about things," says Odejimi. He feels these discussions prepare the students for life later on, on the most basic levels. "If you are on a business trip with a Muslim during Ramadan and you eat in front of him, you might make him feel uncomfortable and not even know it."

Alice Donlan, a graduate of J. E. B. Stuart High in Falls Church, Virginia, feels exposure to many different religions was a positive thing and didn't take away from her own beliefs. "I was raised Episcopalian, my parents are Episcopalian, I went to Stuart High and I'm still Episcopalian," she says. "But it's better to think about other ideas than ignore them. Otherwise you don't really have your own beliefs, just what your parents tell you to believe."

One of the benefits of a diverse environment is that it can foster self-esteem and pride in individual heritage without a feeling of superiority. That seems to be a crucial lesson for our world society. We've felt the direct impact of actions taken under the guise of an extreme belief that there is only one right path. One of the underpinnings of the United States, on the other hand, is the freedom for each of us to practice his own religion and celebrate her own heritage, recognizing that our neighbors deserve the same freedom.

A diverse school with caring leadership provides the ideal environment for students to learn about our precious freedoms, including religious freedom. This works well if students are encouraged to speak from their own perspectives and respect others for doing the same. "We were encouraged to bring our culture and background into the class with us," Sara says. At the private New England college she attended, she often found professors dictating views, with little opportunity for students to question them. "At Annandale we were encouraged to listen to others and dig deeper into our own beliefs."

Exposure to other beliefs and customs doesn't erode our children's sense of who they are. With a firm grounding in the things that are important to their own family, exposure to others can actually strengthen their own identity. To watch your children learn to respect themselves as they grow in their respect for others is one of those cherished moments in parenting.

NOTE

1. TM/© 2002 the Cesar E. Chavez foundation by CMG Worldwide www.cmgww.com

7

MYTH 7

Minority Parents Don't Care about the Education of Their Children

Too often, the social, economic, linguistic, and cultural practices of parents are represented as serious problems rather than valued knowledge. When we reexamine our assumptions about parental absence, we may find our interpretations of parents who care may simply be parents who are like us, parents who feel comfortable in the teachers' domain. Instead of operating on the assumption that absence translates into noncaring, we need to focus on ways to draw parents into the schools.

—Margaret Finders and Cynthia Lewis, "Why Some Parents Don't Come to School"[1]

It's 7:00 P.M. Tuesday night and the parent meeting is about to start. The white mother who leads the group looks around the room. There are only a handful of parents from other ethnic backgrounds present. The other parents grumble under their breath, feeling they have more evidence that minority parents don't care about the education of their children. The principal wrings his hands, wondering why the parents haven't responded to the flyer he sent home in the backpacks yesterday.

"The belief that minority parents don't care couldn't be farther from the truth," says Assistant Principal Roni Silverstein, who has worked in many diverse schools in Montgomery County, Maryland. "When you talk to them you realize that our American schools are the answer to their dreams. What they have had to go through to get their children here is remarkable. Many of them work two or three jobs to stay here. They have the American dream in their hearts. If anything, they care more."

This is supported in a national survey by Public Agenda, a nonprofit public opinion research and education organization. Not only do many minority parents value K–12 education, they feel college is essential for their child. In a survey of African American, Hispanic, and white parents, Public Agenda found that the minority parents actually placed a greater priority on higher education than the white parents.[2]

So why aren't they more visible in the schools? Schools can be an intimidating place for a wide variety of reasons, some relating to language barriers, some cultural, some based on past experience. In the culture of immigrants from Asia or the Pacific Islands, for example, teachers are respected authority figures and parent involvement in school may be viewed as interference.[3] Latino cultures value the welfare of the family above all else, which means Latino parents are reluctant to leave young children home to attend a meeting.[4] For other parents, school is associated with negative experiences, making them distrustful of getting involved.[5]

Eva Midobuche talks about the pain of growing up in the Southwest as a Mexican American, with teachers showing little respect for her or Hispanic culture. "Even the lunchroom was an uncomfortable place. I used to lie about what I had eaten for breakfast. I always said eggs, bacon, toast, milk and orange juice, although I had really eaten something totally different, but just as nutritious."[6]

The overriding issue is that many parents don't feel comfortable in the realm of school.[7] It doesn't mean they don't care about their child's learning; in fact, many are doing all they can to support their child's education at home. "Studies are finding over and over again that minority and low-income parents are just as involved as white middle-class parents in their child's education," says Anne Henderson, author of a series of books summarizing research on family involvement.[8]

Parents are involved at home in a range of ways—from making sure homework is done to monitoring how the student is spending time outside of school, Henderson says. As the students get older, parents often help their children with planning for the future, she says.

However, the traditional parent involvement of talking to teachers and guidance counselors is much more common for middle-class families, particularly white middle-class, says Henderson. "They know how the system works. They don't worry if the school will reject them. They have the information, the skills and a sense of entitlement," Henderson says. "Immigrant families and those with less formal education don't have the experience of navigating the system successfully, so they are less confident entering that realm now," says Henderson, a senior consultant with the Institute for Education and Social Policy at New York University.

The minority parents who are rarely seen because they can't maneuver the American education system are basically just trying to be the best parents they can, like the rest of us. At Annandale High, we conducted a parent survey on issues of interest and concern. The survey was translated into five languages and handed out at Back-to-School Night as well as at a special program held for language-minority parents, which included translators. When the survey results from the English-speaking parents were compared with the responses in other languages, the findings were eye-opening. Across the board, they were nearly identical. High school parents of all backgrounds expressed concern about the same issues, with college selection and financing, peer pressure, and parent-child communication topping the list. The few responses where there was a higher response from language-minority parents reflected their isolation from the broader community. They expressed greater interest in forming parent support groups, and they had a higher level of concern about gangs that often prey on minority teenagers new to the community.

The challenge is for educators and parent leadership to reach out to parents of different ethnic and racial backgrounds and enable them to take an active role in their child's school life, which we now know is a crucial part of a child's educational success. Parent outreach based on the model of the 1960s white suburban school is doomed to failure in today's diverse communities. It simply doesn't build bridges to minority parents. Successful diverse schools around the country, however, have found creative ways to overcome the obstacles and help all parents become the partners in their child's education that they want to be.

Storm Lake, Iowa, like many towns in the United States, watched an influx of immigrants come to take advantage of labor opportunities, changing its population from largely middle-class white in the 1980s to nearly 50 percent minorities today. It wasn't an easy transition, but the school leadership led the way in integrating the new residents into the fabric of the community.

The schools in Storm Lake "put the welcome mat out a foot farther," says Juli Kwikkel, principal of East and West Elementary Schools. Outreach to parents is on a very personal level in Storm Lake. Every new immigrant family is visited at home by school personnel, sometimes Kwikkel herself. Recognizing that parents who work at the nearby packing plant often have trouble attending school events, Kwikkel works with the plant's human resources director to coordinate important programs with parents' shifts schedules.

Since language was a critical barrier for both students and parents, the school marshaled community resources to offer language and parenting skills for parents in one section of the school. Iowa Central Community College and the elementary schools provided the instructors. School board meetings were publicized in both print notices and radio announcements in multiple languages.

The whole town has grown from the experience of building a multicultural community. "People in Storm Lake don't talk about separation anymore the way they did a few years ago. Today people are talking about things like building a new community center instead of who's moving into the neighborhood," says Kwikkel.

In Boston, schools that are part of the successful Boston Excels program offer a variety of programs for parents, including family literacy classes, monthly home visits, and family field trips. They have seen a dramatic increase in school-parent connections. "We're building parent engagement though family literacy," says Susan Klaw, Excels Family Literacy director.

Parents who participate in the family literacy program at Boston's Otis School write autobiographies. One father from El Salvador wrote:

To be honest, I never thought I was going to learn so much in the Family School. Besides English, I have learned how to help my children in school. The monthly tips, "Helping Children Learn," have been an important tool for me also to understand what to do and at what age. Now we talk a lot more. They ask me more and I feel glad about it. To understand

my children's school was also a short-term goal for me. I have been doing
many things: opening the doors and welcoming people to the school; visiting my children's classrooms more often; talking to teachers in general.
I'm satisfied with the way I've been treated at school. I know many of the
teachers' names now and what they are doing or what class they teach. But
most of all, my kids feel a lot more confident in school. Their progress has
increased a lot.

The story of parents getting involved once they have been empow-
ered to do so is seen over and over again in diverse schools around the
country:

- In Lincolnton, North Carolina, PTA leadership worked with the
  school leadership to put together a school improvement team
  that included a parent of Hispanic decent who was bilingual. A
  broad-based outreach program includes home visits, translation
  of newsletters and other parent information, and distribution of
  parenting videos in Spanish.
- In Binghamton, New York, Woodrow Wilson Elementary School
  invites parents into school through one-on-one invitations. To work
  around language barriers the school uses translators or a bilingual
  community member, or even an older brother or sister more advanced in English.
- In Beverly Hills, California, the high school sponsors a Pancake
  Breakfast Welcome for families of students who are not native
  English speakers. The principal serves the pancakes and then
  talks with the families about their needs. Throughout the year,
  the school has translators available for all parent communications in Farsi, Hebrew, Spanish, Korean, and Russian. An international parents committee seeks ways they can support the
  school.

In a country where nearly everyone came as an immigrant, we must remember those who helped our grandparents and great-great-grandparents
become a part of this society. I was very close to my grandparents who fled
Russia after family members had been killed in the state-sanctioned
pogroms. My mother entered kindergarten speaking only Yiddish. My

grandfather went to night school to learn English for the work world, but my grandmother could neither read nor write English. Neither of them stepped foot in their children's school, because it was too foreign, too frightening; but no one cared about education more than they did. Both their children earned college degrees.

We need to let go of the myth that minority parents don't care about their children. We know a lot more about the key role that parents play in their child's education today than we did in my grandparents' day. We need to make sure we are finding ways for ethnic and racial minority parents to feel comfortable and valued in their child's school. I have spoken at minority parent meetings with multiple translators provided, watching the light in the parents' eyes as they feel a part of a larger school community. I have seen parents proudly bring their favorite food to an International Dinner and pose for photos of the whole extended family in native garb, seated in the school cafeteria where they had never ventured before. I have heard parents engage the principal in concerned dialogue when he left the school building and visited their community.

Following school policies that create obstacles to minority parent involvement, and then criticizing them for not becoming involved, keeps us all from achieving the American dream. That dream is not just a home and a car, but a community where whole families live and learn and respect each other. We all grow from a school community that reflects the involvement of parents of many different backgrounds.

NOTES

1. Margaret Finders and Cynthia Lewis, "Why Some Parents Don't Come to School," *Educational Leadership* 51, no. 8 (May 1994): 50–52.

2. John Immerwahr with Tony Foleno, "Great Expectations: How the Public and Parents—White, African American and Hispanic—View Higher Education," *Public Agenda* (May 2000): 4.

3. Wendy Schwartz, "A Guide to Communicating with Asian American Families," *ERIC Clearinghouse on Urban Education* (New York: Teachers College). http://eric-web.tc.Columbia.edu/guides/pg2.html [accessed 15 June 2002].

4. Wendy Schwartz, "Strategies for Improving the Educational Outcomes of Latinas," *ERIC Clearinghouse on Urban Education*, no. 167 (October 2001), EDO-UD-01-6 (New York: Teachers College).

5. Renee White-Clark and Larry E. Decker, *The "Hard-To-Reach" Parent: Old Challenges, New Insights*, 1996, http://eric-web.tc.columbia.edu/families/ hard_to_reach/chapter1.html#parent [accessed 15 June 2002].

6. Eva Midobuche, "Respect in the Classroom: Reflections of a Mexican–American Educator," *Educational Leadership* 56, no. 7 (April 1999): 80–82.

7. Jorge Ruiz-de-Velasco and Michael Fix, *Overlooked and Underserved: Immigrant Children in U.S. Secondary Schools* (Washington, D.C.: Urban Institute, 2001), 63.

8. See Anne Henderson and Karen L. Mapp, *A New Wave of Evidence: The Impact of School, Family, and Community on Student Achievement* (Austin, Tex.: Educational Development Laboratory, 2002).

II

THE REALITIES OF DIVERSE SCHOOLS
AND OF OUR SOCIETY

"Face," by Mohamed Elmubarak

SCHOOL REALITY I

Students with Different Backgrounds and Experiences Bring New Insights to the Classroom

A racially diverse student body . . . contributes to the robust exchange of ideas which is so essential to a quality system of education.

—Bredhoff & Kaiser, P.L.L.C., *The Benefits of a Racially-Diverse
Student Body in Elementary/Secondary Education*[1]

It's the beginning of the second quarter in 12th grade American government class at Annandale High. Jennifer Burns, who left her congres-
sional staff job to teach high school, presents several views on a Utopian
government. She randomly assigns the students into groups for a coop-
erative learning project. The assignment: delve into one aspect of a
Utopian government.

Within five minutes of discussing the assignment, students in my son
Alex's group realized that there were five religious perspectives represented within their group of six students: fundamentalist Protestant, Jewish, Catholic, Sikh, and Muslim. Within another five minutes, they knew
what they would work on: the relationship between church and state.

Can you imagine the richness of the discussions among those students? Alex was so enthused about the project that he couldn't wait to
get into class and discuss the issues with his peers. Not only did they
hear different messages at the respective houses of worship, they had

far different life experiences filtering their views. They each researched their own religious heritage, as well as others, to be well informed during the discussions. They wrestled with issues that many adults never consider. If the government were to mandate putting the Ten Commandments in every classroom, would it be the version used by the Catholic, the Protestant, or the Jew, which actually differ in how they are interpreted and numbered? If this country was founded on Judeo-Christian principles, as many leaders state, where does that leave the Sikh and the Muslim? If the Supreme Court of the land has decreed that a crèche is a secular, not a religious, symbol, why would the Jew and the Sikh never have one in their homes?

The students decided that their Utopian government would have no preferred religion, as many felt the United States did. As part of their class presentation, they created a flag that included the symbols of all their religions. Others in their class disagreed with the analysis they presented, providing more thought-provoking dialogue.

Discussions like that are not unusual at Annandale High. Students are encouraged to speak their minds and then listen to and respect what others say. This leads to fascinating discourse where students defend their own positions, yet learn to have open minds. It would be wonderful if young minds in every school could have the opportunity to practice this kind of diplomacy. What training for the dialogue among people from other countries with other perspectives that is certain to be a crucial part of their lives when they are adults.

Social studies teachers are at a particular advantage at a diverse school like Annandale. Recent immigrants bring firsthand knowledge of life in distant lands, plus they often have an appreciation for the freedoms and bounty of the United States that American-born students may take for granted.

Alex Berens, now in his mid-20s, vividly remembers the discussions in his freshman world history class. He marvels at his teacher's ability to get everyone to present a different perspective on the historical and current events discussed in class, thus encouraging each student to think critically. "The teacher never presented a definitive answer, just question after question. Mr. Waters used people like paints to draw the different sides of an argument. I might not have agreed with everyone, but it raised a lot of ideas I hadn't contemplated before."

Diversity enlivens so many other areas of study, as well. English teacher Virginia Crowley's classes at Annandale High discuss the essays known as "Letters from an American Farmer," penned by Jean de Crèvecoeur in 1782. He defines an American as a "descendent of Europeans" who chose to come to this land. If he was "honest, sober and industrious," he could prosper in a welcoming land of opportunity, according to de Crèvecoeur.

Crowley assigns the students the task of exploring their own immigration to this country, and then compare and contrast their family story with de Crèvecoeur's letters. If they don't have knowledge of their families immigration pattern, they can interview someone else. They edit their papers in small groups. The students find that many of their families' stories differ from de Crèvecoeur's view that immigration is based solely on free will. In some cases, the high schoolers remember coming to the country as young children, having no choice in the matter. Many of their parents left to escape armed conflicts or threatening political conditions, truly not wanting to leave their homelands. "The different backgrounds bring us a wealth of material to discuss," says Crowley.

Teacher Katharine Johnson has had similar experiences when discussing immigration patterns with her second grade class in Portland, Oregon. She sees students push themselves to learn more, often reading books beyond their level, because they are inspired by the in-depth discussions of culture.

The range of views and backgrounds inspires students to think deeper in nearly every subject. Chemistry teacher Tom Pratuch watched a fascinating discourse evolve when he began a discussion on the importance of chemistry to society with his Annandale High students. The students explored the chemistry of food, both natural and after processing. This led to a discussion of how food additives, as well as pharmaceuticals and cosmetics, are tested to make sure they are safe.

Some students championed animal rights, asserting that animals should never be used to test for human safety. One student who had recently fled the starvation of an African country looked mystified by the entire discussion. "Animal rights? What are 'animal rights?' he asked with genuine puzzlement. "Animals are food." The other students, most of whom had never known an empty dinner plate or seen a farm animal, stopped to think. They didn't know how to respond with the respect his comments deserved. Several came up to Pratuch after class to tell him that the discussion had forced them to think about animals in an entirely new context. "We were so used to thinking about animals one way and not thinking there could be any other way," one student said.

Every teacher in a vibrant diverse school can tell you stories of the striking contributions of students from ethnic and racial minorities, who in turn inspire new insights from others in the class. Geometry teacher Donna Erickson talks about her "Quilt Project," an innovative alternative assessment activity that has received national attention.[2] The assignment helps students develop an understanding and appreciation for geometry and symmetry, she says. Each student creates original templates, calculates the area of all the shapes in their patches, and describes the various symmetries. The students work with a significant adult in their lives, usually a parent, but occasionally another teacher.

A critical part of the project is creation of a "family block." One of the templates in the students' quilts must depict their family in at least two significant ways: their ethnic heritage, special memories, personalities of favorite family members, significant events, or important traditions. The students write an essay about the family block, from a geometrical and symbolic viewpoint, and make a presentation to the class.

Erickson's voice becomes choked with emotion as she discusses the day the students make their presentations at Annandale High. "I never had that kind of reaction when I did this at schools with homogeneous populations. It was just another project. Here it is totally different," she says. Assigned late in the year when the students are comfortable with each other, "incredible stories come out," she says.

Erickson tells of Minh who hand sewed 64 tiny squares together with a large red heart in the center, representing her father. When she left Vietnam, Minh never told her father she loved him, and she didn't realize she would never have the opportunity to tell him in the future. She told the class that the quilt gave her a way to tell her dad that she remembers him and loves him. The class fell silent with Minh.

Other students recall their homelands with colorful fabrics reminiscent of the flags of countries from all over the globe. Erickson has seen squares with memories of Colombia, Cambodia, Pakistan, China, Vietnam, Nigeria, Morocco, Mexico, Scotland, Poland, Bolivia, Ireland, England, Belgium, Ethiopia, Algeria, Italy, Afghanistan, Korea, and Brazil. Inspired by their classmates' heartfelt stories, students of all different backgrounds make the quilts a meaningful representation of their families. Ann called her square "faith" because "it was the main thing that kept my family together . . . not just faith in God, but in each other." Frank's quilt included a triangle of light purple with dark purple flowers to represent his grandmother "because she had a beautiful garden and spent much time in it."

Some schools build on their cultures and ethnic backgrounds to inspire discussions schoolwide. Walnut Hill Elementary School in Dallas plays music connected to a theme or holiday each morning over the public address system. On Cinco de Mayo, the students may hear mariachi music, or songs about dreidles during Chanukah, according to teacher Jeri Kitner. If the students are working on the character trait of respect, administrators may play Aretha Franklin's "Respect" to get the conversations started. Students from the different backgrounds can use their own cultural heritage to enlighten others about the theme for the day.

Research supports the notion that all students benefit academically from a diverse environment simply because different students bring different skills and ideas to the classroom. Social scientists have found that groups with different races and ethnic backgrounds are better at creative problem solving than are homogeneous groups.[3] It makes clear sense to me.

It's time we stopped believing the myth that only minority students benefit from being in a mixed student body. All students benefit from the insights of those who challenge their thinking and inspire them to clarify their own perspectives. That's one of the reasons that so many students who attended diverse public schools come back and thank their parents after they leave the nest. They realize what a priceless gift they received—not just knowledge, but insight and wisdom.

NOTES

1. Bredhoff & Kaiser, P.L.L.C. *The Benefits of a Racially-Diverse Student Body in Elementary/Secondary Education* (Washington, D.C.: National Education Association, 1999).

2. Donna Erickson, "Geometry Teacher's 'Project Quilt Day' Leads to 'More Than I Bargained For!'" *Alpha Delta KAPPAN* (December 2000): 21–23.

3. Bredhoff & Kaiser, P.L.L.C., *The Benefits of a Racially-Diverse Student Body*, 4.

9

SCHOOL REALITY 2

Students Who Closely Interact with People from Different Backgrounds Learn That Reality Extends beyond Their Own Limited Experiences

> Instead of responding to rising diversity with fear and insecurity, we can treat our diversity as an asset and devise ways of responding to it which enable our society to reap benefits from our pluralism.
>
> —Pedro Noguera, "Confronting the Challenge of Diversity"[1]

As parents, our first instinct is to protect our children. We want them to be comfortable and successful and, of course, happy. So we teach them how to behave and what to believe, guiding them toward the right path. In an effort to build their self-esteem and make sure they stay on that path, we can create a cocoon, surrounding them with people who confirm that they think and act correctly—"good" people acting the "right" way. Sometimes, however, we keep that cocoon in place long after our children should be flapping their wings and flying away to new experiences.

Sooner or later our children are exposed to lots of good people who don't act or think exactly the same way. The question will be whether they are open to that concept or frightened and intimidated by it. Will they learn from others, or try reweaving that cocoon to keep out any new information?

I admit I am sensitive to this concept as a member of a religious minority. I believe deeply in my Jewish faith and am an active member of the Jewish community. I have spoken to educated people who do not have the most basic knowledge about my religion or my customs. They have never felt the need to do so, since they are Christian people living in a largely Christian society where they can easily ignore anyone else. But by limiting your knowledge to people who are like you, you limit your world, fostering misperceptions caused by ignorance and fear. When my husband was a student teacher in 1973 in Arlington County, Virginia, just outside of Washington, D.C., the parents of one of his students asked him where his horns were when she found out he was Jewish. Unfortunately, many of our Jewish friends have had similar experiences.

Students who attend diverse schools, however, quickly learn how people view the world through a variety of prisms. At Annandale High, students know that January 1st isn't the only new year. They learn from their classmates that Asian cultures celebrate the lunar new year in January or February; that the Jewish new year of Rosh Hashana in the fall is a religious, not a secular holiday; and that Norooz is the Persian new year welcoming spring. When students' eyes are opened to new worlds, they open their minds to new approaches, new ways of thinking. And they are more accepting of people who are different, realizing they are not necessarily bad, just different.

Students in diverse schools learn that you can show respect for someone who is different from you while respecting yourself. Beverly Hills High School has a large percentage of recent immigrants from Iran. Norooz is a major holiday in their culture, usually celebrated with a large family gathering in the evening. Principal Ben Bushman schedules a professional development day for teachers on the day after Norooz. Thus the students can celebrate with their families and not worry about getting up early for school the next day. Most Christians never have to think about what it is like to go to school on one of their major holidays. Yet every student at Beverly Hills High is now sensitized to how difficult it can be to follow practices that are different from the dominant culture. As adults their eyes will be open to those around them who are following different, but equally important, customs.

An Annandale High, every student knows about Ramadan. Students have great respect for their Muslim friends who go to school for a month, fasting from sunup to sundown. No one resents the fact that Muslim students have a study hall during lunch so they don't have to enter the cafeteria.

Now that I have met observant Muslims, I often think about the difficulty of fasting an entire month, particularly when they are going against the tide of the dominant culture. When Ramadan falls in December, Muslims benefit from the shortest hours of sunlight. But on the other hand, they must be part of a society that is in the midst of lavish celebrations. Standing in line in the bank in late December, I couldn't help but appreciate how hard it was for one of the bank officials, a Muslim woman with her head covered, as her branch set out festive dishes of food on every table.

Jamilah Alzer, a graduate of Annandale High, says that going to a diverse school has connected her personally to what is happening far from her own home. "It matters to me what's going on in other countries. After going to school with kids from different places, I know these people. More of my feelings are involved. When you hear about South Africa, you sympathize with the people. But when you know somebody from there and you understand what's going on, you can empathize."

It is important for our students to be exposed to lives other than their own to truly gain an appreciation for their own lives. Many middle-class parents worry that in our zeal to give our children all the things we want for them—sometimes the things we didn't have in our own youth—we are raising children who believe they are simply entitled to so much. This negates the ethic that you must earn what you have or even that you appreciate what you have been given.

I have found that exposure to many students who have struggled for everything in their lives has given my children a new appreciation for what they have. That's a different view than what they learned in their fairly homogeneous elementary school. About two thirds of the students in our neighborhood elementary school were from newer neighborhoods with bigger houses. My kids complained our kitchen wasn't modern enough; our furniture not as classy. My comments that they were indeed privileged to live in an affluent community in one of the most affluent countries in the world fell on deaf ears.

All that changed when they went to a regional middle school. They were suddenly face-to-face with children who had recently left countries facing starvation or lived in dismal refugee camps. As they became friends with these students, my children began to see that these peers had the same hopes and cares that they did, but they had not had the same advantages. Sara and Alex began to realize how lucky they were to have a full refrigerator, new clothes, and their own quiet rooms.

This appreciation of lives beyond their own continued to grow through high school. On Friday nights when many of the kids went on to parties after the football games, one of Alex's friends often left after their band performance to help out in his father's dry cleaning business. A star of the football team could be seen walking several miles home after practice on weekdays because he had no one in his family who could pick him up, let alone give him his own car.

I have heard similar stories from other parents at Annandale as well. Liz Segall says:

> In addition to the strong academic program, Annandale High has the advantage of giving my children the opportunity to be with other teenagers from a wide range of income levels, races, religions and cultures. My three daughters watched their classmates work to help support their families and take on the responsibility for the care of their younger siblings. They listened to the stories of the tremendous danger and effort other families went through just to come to the United States. My daughters gradually began to lose their feelings of entitlement which they had unwittingly developed in their homogenous middle-class elementary school, and began to understand in a way that no book could fully explain to them their unusually privileged place in the world. No one can convince me that there is a better education than that.

Annandale High graduate Alex Berens remains amazed at how others of his generation do not have the same appreciation. In college he talked to a fellow student who was thrilled that he would be able to drop all his classes that semester without his poor grades being reflected on his GPA. "Can you get a refund for your classes?" Berens asked him. "No, but it won't show up on my record!" he replied. Berens was appalled that this student didn't care he had just wasted thousands of dollars.

Our children grow so much when their perceptions are tested by those around them. They learn that there are many ways to view the world, countless perspectives worth hearing. They have a deeper appreciation of who they are, when held up to the light of who others are. And they realize that other lives have just as much meaning as their own.

NOTE

1. Pedro Noguera, "Confronting the Challenge of Diversity," *School Administrator* 56, no. 5 (May 1999): 16–18

10

SCHOOL REALITY 3

Sterotypes and Prejudice Break Down When
Students Have Personal Contact with Members
of Other Races and Cultures

As the country becomes more multiracial every year, the schools face
the challenge of a level of multiracial diversity never before seen in
American society. The extremely strong focus on evaluating schools
only in terms of standardized test scores in two or three subject areas
may have distracted attention from a function of schools that is vital to
the future of American society and American democracy. As the only
institution that reaches the great majority of young people (nearly
nine-tenths of U.S. children attend public schools), this function is of
great importance for the future of U.S. society. Given public school-
ing's unique role in the United States, it is important to understand
how they are helping or hindering the preparation of students to live
and work among people different from themselves.

—*The Impact of Racial and Ethnic Diversity on Educational Outcomes, Cambridge, MA, School District*, Civil Rights Project[1]

In the best tradition of American education, school is the place where
all students learn essential information to become part of the wider
American society. They are not only educated in "readin', writin', and
'rithmetic," but also in the values that form the foundation of our society. There are few more important lessons for the future of our society
than a reduction in prejudice.

"Breaking down stereotypes is much easier in a diverse school," says Annandale High School Principal Donald Clausen. "The opportunities are everywhere."

Classrooms can be a breeding ground of understanding in a diverse school. "Literature is a wonderful vehicle for bringing out cultural differences, which sometimes ironically, are not so different," says Virginia Crowley, an English teacher at Annandale High. When there are allusions to the Old Testament in the literature, she makes a point of explaining the references since some in her class did not grow up with the Judeo-Christian Bible. "The kids begin to bring in their own religious traditions. We find there are many similarities. For example, they all have creation stories, systems of rewards for good and punishment for bad, consequences for actions, an afterlife," Crowley says.

"These are rich, rich conversations," Crowley says. "The kids ask each other questions. Sometimes they think about it and bring back another question. Once in a while it goes back to the dinner table and they learn more from their parents. The discussions are rich for everybody and it really does promote cultural understanding."

James Logan High School in Union City, California, offers students the opportunity to study together in rigorous academies. Language arts teacher Trish Tripepi talks about her own enlightenment as she watched the Electronic Media Academy take shape during its initial year in 1997–1998. Fifty students entered the program that integrates the academic courses of language arts and social science with multimedia and video production.

James Logan is a comprehensive high school of more than 4,000 students who speak more than 25 languages, located on the east side of the San Francisco Bay. "None of the teachers in the academy core knew what to expect that first year," Tripepi says, "but what we got was a diverse mix of cultures, ethnicities, interests, skill levels, and motivation."

What they also got was a group of students who began to see beyond color or accent to the heart of the individual. Working in groups, "natural leaders began to emerge to ensure that the results of the projects reflected the best work of each individual member," Tripepi says. "Innate talents were discovered; it was quickly determined who could most creatively prepare a storyboard, who could best lay down a musical background for a slide show, who could operate the videocameras," she says. "All the students had something to share and something to contribute."

"Race, cultural differences, and intelligence were no longer an issue. What mattered most was working together to create a project of which *every* group member could be proud," Tripepi says. The experiences of the students "strongly illustrate how stereotypes can be broken down because of daily interactions among students of different races and ethnic backgrounds," she says.

The academy students remained together as a group for two years, sharing the same core classes in the morning. "They emerged from the program as mature, responsible adults who had gained an appreciation for each others' contributions and abilities," Tripepi states. A great many of them have gone on to pursue careers in multimedia, video production, broadcasting, or related fields. Logan High still offers this academy and several others.

Annandale High graduate Jaspreet Singh, now in his 20s, found the diversity in his secondary schools particularly valuable.

> In the adolescent phase of life, there is a mindset that you need to be part of something "normal," whatever that might be. Annandale High and schools like it try to change that mindset by creating an environment that encourages you to be who you are, share who you are, and learn about others. You begin to realize, "I am as much a part of this society as any American and I also have things about me that I should be proud of."

Diverse schools offer educators many teachable moments. Leila Meyerratken teaches foreign languages to middle schoolers in Lafayette, Indiana, a town with a recent influx of Hispanic families. She was concerned about the negative behavior of some of her Caucasian students toward the Hispanics. "A teacher's attentiveness to the conduct of her students and how they interact with each other is an opportunity for learning," Meyerratken says. When she pointed out to her beginning Spanish class that many of the recent immigrant families faced a language barrier in their new county, her class came up with the idea for a two-year bilingual calendar.

They quickly set to work on a comprehensive calendar including practical information for newcomers in Spanish with a translation of important words in English. The bottom of each calendar page explains customs or traditions of Spanish speakers from different countries. The students sought information from a variety of resources, from parents to local community organizations and the nearby university. Students illustrated the calendar with their own poems and pictures of welcome and friendship. With funding from the Indiana Humanities Council and the Indiana Department of Education, plus cash donations from some local agencies, the class was able to print and distribute 600 calendars.

One of the greatest values of the calendar was the newfound respect her students had for each other. "Through the calendar, the students were able to work together and learn acceptance," Meyerratken says.

Diverse classrooms in the primary grades offer opportunities to affect attitudes before they are tainted by prejudice. Kindergarten teacher Donna Schutz asks each of her students to do a family album with their parents. When they bring in their album, they get to place their picture on the map to show where they were born. Then they attach a piece of yarn from the location of their school in Springfield, Virginia, to the photo. The students quickly learn they are part of a world community. "They just accept that he's from Peru, he's from Pakistan, and she's from Pennsylvania," she says.

Young children rapidly accept the different dress and names of others, without the judgments that form later in life. I remember when my son came back from first grade talking about a new student, Gidithar. "Is he from India?" I asked. Alex looked surprised at my amazing knowledge and said, "How did you know!" To him, Gidithar was as ordinary a name as Jennifer or Mike.

Students who go to well-run diverse schools often find their minds are so accepting of difference, their optimism astounds outsiders. Students from Annandale High's advanced placement history class were invited to appear on ABC's *Good Morning America* in January 2002 to discuss the influences of the television series *Roots*, which is used in their classroom by teacher Eleanor Shumaker. The students, who were from a wide mix of races and ethnic backgrounds, agreed that America had come very far in the twenty years since the program was first telecast, and that we could expect great progress in the next twenty years.

One of the students mentioned in passing that race isn't an issue with 99 percent of Annandale's student body. Interviewer George Stephanopoulos was stunned by that statement. He stopped the discussion and said, "Wait a minute, do you all agree?" The students thought for a moment and then nonchalantly nodded their heads in agreement. They didn't even realize this was a startling view.

Some students find the environment so positive, they worry what they will find once they move on. Trish Tripepi recalls judging a competition at California's Logan High for seniors who were applying for a memorial award. One of the questions the candidates were asked was, "How has Logan's diversity prepared you for the real world?" While one girl stated that Logan "makes me more prepared because I'll be able to interact with the people I meet on an equal, more tolerant level," another noted her concern that Logan doesn't represent broader society. "Out there, there's more prejudice and hatred and intolerance, and I think I'm going to be saddened by the reality of life."

For the most part, however, students relish their years in an environment where they interact daily with people who come from a wide variety of backgrounds. Often they don't realize what a gift it was until after they have left. Annandale High parent Jamie Bacigalupi recalls her oldest son calling home from college one day. He was attending a predominantly white university where many of the students had graduated from schools filled with students just like them. He was shocked at their lack of knowledge about others. "He called to thank me for sending him to a high school where there are kids from different countries, with different religions, with different skin colors," says Bacigalupi.

My daughter, Sara, struck a similar chord.

> When there are only a few minorities, as there were at my college, they were "exotic" in the eyes of white students who had no earlier exposure to them. For the most part, the white students viewed them as interesting, but not people they could connect with. At Annandale High, it wasn't trendy or cool to be a minority, it was just an accepted part of who you are.

Sara took several college classes on racial issues in America. "No one, not even the teachers, felt there could be an environment where you are race-aware, but not racist. But it exists at Annandale High."

Alice Donlan, who graduated from Fairfax County's J. E. B. Stuart High—a school with students from seventy countries, featured in *National Geographic*[2]—saw the benefits of attending a school that she says represented "basically the world" even before her college classes began. Donlan was pleased to find out her college roommate was half Palestinian. "I was happy that she was from a culture different than mine. I was glad she wasn't the stereotypical white teeny-bopper who doesn't know about anyone besides herself." Her roommate was similarly happy when she met Donlan. She had attended a predominantly white high school a few miles from Stuart where she had experienced jeers from other students. Donlan says, "She was so happy that I didn't think she was going to be a terrorist and that I knew about Ramadan."

As I talk to students who graduated from well-run diverse schools, I am struck by the common response that they feel sorry for students from nearly all-white schools. Alex Berens remembers coming back to his alma mater to watch the Annandale High boys' lacrosse team battle their way to the state championship. "I was amazed to see the different races on a team for what has traditionally been a 'white sport'—Vietnamese, Cambodian, African American, Latino—lots of kids from mixed backgrounds. Then I looked at the nearly all-white teams from the other schools. They really missed out on something."

Sometimes the former students are hit in the face with the misperceptions of people who didn't have the advantage of sitting side by side with people of other cultures. Jaspreet Singh is a neighborhood kid to his friends, a trumpeter who won awards for his talent in high school, and a leader in the marching band at the University of Michigan, where he earned his engineering degree. Yet many who don't know him, or any other Sikhs, only see his turban and full beard.

Jaspreet talks of going out for a birthday dinner with a friend from work and several others who joined the celebration. They went to a restaurant where the waiters entertain between courses. Jaspreet requested a song from the show *42nd Street*, one of his favorites when he played in the orchestra pit for the school plays. He found out the next day that one of the guests who didn't know him was surprised that someone who looked like Jaspreet could possibly know about American Broadway tunes.

When students spend most of their day together in an environment that promotes tolerance and acceptance, it's hard to maintain old prejudices. The stereotypes simply fall by the wayside when challenged by the reality of daily experiences. How lucky we would be if every student—and every adult—could have these experiences.

NOTES

1. *The Impact of Racial and Ethnic Diversity on Educational Outcomes, Cambridge, MA, School District* (Cambridge, Mass.; Civil Rights Project, Harvard University, 2002).

2. Joel L. Swerdlow, "Changing America," *National Geographic* (September 2001), 43–61.

SOCIETY REALITY I

Our Youth Must Learn How to Actively Participate in a Diverse National and International Society

> We do all our students a disservice when we prepare them to live in a society that no longer exists. Given the tremendous diversity in our society, it makes eminent good sense to educate all our students to be comfortable with differences.
>
> —Sonia Nieto, "What Does It Mean to Affirm Diversity?"[1]

Like it or not, our children face an interactive world society. The Internet, high-speed mobile computers, cell phones—technology as familiar to today's youth as transistor radios were to their parents—make rapid communication around the globe not only possible, but probable. The global economy is a reality. What happens in the Japanese and European stock markets daily affects U.S. markets. We can buy goods or sell services internationally at the click of a mouse.

In addition to our economic ties to far-away lands, we have painfully learned that we are connected to people around the world in ways we barely considered before September 11, 2001. People who have had little direct contact with the United States or its residents can change our society irreparably. We need to have a basic understanding of how other communities in the world think and operate.

We don't even need to go beyond our shores to see that our youth must be able to interact with people of different backgrounds. By the year 2050 Caucasians will be only a slight majority of the population. Today's students will be the employees in tomorrow's more diverse workforce. They deserve an education that will help them become effective staff, colleagues, and bosses in a workplace that is filled with people of different backgrounds and different perspectives.

We can't adequately prepare children for the future if they come in contact only with people like themselves. Our children can hold strong beliefs, but they must be broad thinkers, able to dialogue with those who have another perspective. They must develop the skills to interact with people who grew up in far different circumstances, and learn how to identify similarities and respect differences. Diverse schools provide a unique learning lab for this crucial education.

Diverse schools provide opportunities for students of different backgrounds and races and ethnic groups to interact in class, in the hallways, and after school. At Annandale High, as in many diverse schools, students do sit in mixed groups in the lunchroom and hang out with each other on weekends. "There were lots of Middle-Eastern students that I could have segregated myself with at lunch," says Jamilah Alzer, "but that just didn't happen. I had classes with different people, and had gone through elementary and junior high with them, so it just wasn't an issue."

Talk to anyone with a student at a well-run diverse school and you are likely get an earful about the personal growth of their child. Debbie Simons can see the positive influences of a diverse school on her daughter who is only in second grade. Simons sends her daughter to Side by Side Community School, a charter school in Norwalk, Connecticut, with an urban-suburban population that crosses many races, cultures, and economic groups. Although Side by Side is located in one of the poorest neighborhoods in Norwalk, Simons believes the school provides her daughter distinct advantages. "My child is enriched. I don't see my daughter restricted in her relationships. I see her more accepting of each person. She has learned a lot about the different foods children eat, different languages they speak, and the cultural and traditional practices."

Simons believes this diverse education will open doors for her daughter all her life. "My child will succeed in all environments. My child will

survive among all ethnic groups. She doesn't see boundaries I saw growing up."

Simons's vision of the advantages she is providing her daughter are
confirmed by parents of students who have graduated from diverse public schools and gone on to college and careers. Vic Meyers, the superintendent of Harrison School District No. 2 in Colorado Springs, Colorado, sees the personal growth in the graduates of his system, including
his own children. "All three of my children were well prepared for college, not just academically, but also in their ability to interact with other
students." Meyers remembers the ten-year reunion for his daughter's
high school class, when many students gathered at his home. "We had
many discussions about how comfortable they felt with other cultures
and ethnic groups." They witnessed others at college and in the workplace who had "built-in fear and intimidation" of people from different
backgrounds. The kids from Harrison just didn't have those problems.

Betty Paschall, PTA president at S. Ray Lowder School in Lincolnton,
North Carolina, can describe the difference she sees in her youngest
child, the only one of her three to attend a diverse school. "She has
learned to be more open to learning, to ask more questions, and to not
be afraid to interact with different people."

Jan Patton, who served on the school board in Storm Lake, Iowa, as
the demographics changed from nearly all white to about half ethnic
minorities in the 1990s, sees her children and grandchildren reaping the
benefits of the new diversity. "Our kids in grade school are experiencing
other cultures in their home town instead of having to wait until they
leave for college or move away as adults," Patton says. "My third grandson came home from school and proclaimed, 'Grandma, I can say *red* in
three languages!' Isn't that wonderful?"

Students' increased ability to work with others of varying backgrounds
has been documented by the Harvard Civil Rights Project in several surveys of teenagers who attend diverse high schools around the country.[2]
"We're finding strikingly consistent responses," says Gary Orfield. "They
understand each other, have friends along racial lines, are comfortable
talking with each other, and are comfortable asking questions about difficult issues. They plan to live together in interracial communities."

One of the lessons our society has learned is that a school must become a place where students learn to accept those who aren't their mir-

ror image. We've seen too many violent assaults against students who didn't fit the dominant mold, and horrible attacks by youth feeling devalued and disenfranchised. That lesson of acceptance is much easier to teach in diverse schools than those with only one population group.

Diane Brody says she realized what a special place her local diverse elementary school is when her son was in kindergarten in 1986. He developed an autoimmune skin disease called *alopecia areata* and within a year had lost all the hair on his head. The administrators at Groveton Elementary School in Fairfax County, Virginia, let him wear a baseball cap even though there was a no-hat rule, "but he finally just took his hat off and didn't care," says Brody. The other students didn't even notice anything different about him.

> The kids just saw this kid is brown, this one is black, this one has a turban, and this one has no hair. I took him to a few conventions so he could meet other kids with the same condition. We heard horror stories about reactions of students in other schools, including special private schools. I came away with a real appreciation for the power of a diverse classroom. I could not have paid for him to go to any school in the country to have a better experience than he did.

Mary Mason, president of the board of directors of a grade 7–12 charter school in Grand Rapids, Michigan, notes there is a "culture of acceptance of individual quirks and lack of cliques" at their diverse school. Students who might not be part of the mainstream culture in a homogeneous school feel they have a place and can contribute something. "People are not so much accepted at Gateway in spite of their quirks, but they are appreciated because of their individuality," Mason said.

At schools like Annandale High, it's hard to feel you are "different" because there is no dominant culture. Yes, athletes are heralded, but the football stars are Asian, Middle Eastern, African American, and Hispanic, as well as Caucasian. A girl of Indian heritage wins accolades for her portrayal of Helen Keller in the school play, a Hispanic boy plays a convincing Tevya in *Fiddler on the Roof*, and an African American boy teaches the other chorus students how to sway to a Gospel piece. Student government leaders such as Nabeela and Vihn work side by side with Jason and Katie.

This important respect for people as individuals can be crucial when emotions are high. When Muslims and Sikhs became targets of violence on American streets after the terrorist attacks in the fall of 2001, diverse schools around the country proved to be safe havens.

Seizing the opportunity to teach a crucial life lesson in the aftermath of the terrorist attacks, Principal Donald Clausen reminded his students of the unique learning environment they enjoyed. He started the morning announcements on September 13, 2001, at Annandale High School, a school only a few miles from the Pentagon with students from more than eight-five nations, with words that acknowledged the great loss of a few days earlier and added a challenge to his students:

> We must not allow this terror to drive us away from being the people we are called to be. We assert the vision of community, tolerance, compassion, justice, and the sacredness of human life, which lies at the heart of all our traditions. America must be a safe place for all our citizens in all their diversity. It is especially important that our citizens who share national origins, ethnicity, or religion with whomever attacked us are, themselves, protected among us. . . . It is up to us at Annandale High School as a microcosm of the world to demonstrate, indeed to be shining examples to the world, of how peoples from many backgrounds, cultures, and countries can work and play together peacefully and cooperatively. . . . We need to show the world how important it is to build understanding among people, people who may start out thinking they have absolutely nothing in common, learn otherwise, and are completely changed. How lucky we are to have such rich life experiences.

The students of Annandale High met that challenge, as they do every day. Annandale High graduate Jamilah Alzer says her freshman brother had no problem attending the school after the attacks. In another environment, he might have feared reprisals as a Muslim with the name Mohammed. But at Annandale, he had many friends of different backgrounds from his classes as well as from the football and basketball teams.

Diverse schools around the nation similarly reported very few incidents or threats of violence, serving as role models for the greater society. Students know fellow students as individuals, with names and personalities, refraining from snap judgments because their peers' religion or style of dress resembled the attackers. What teachers did see were many students reaching out to reassure their Muslim classmates.

But that's what life is all about at a diverse school. They see members of different races and ethnic groups as equals, with few barriers between them. They respect and celebrate each others' cultures.

One of my favorite memories is from my daughter's senior prom. We volunteered to host a breakfast for the group of twelve who went together. In addition to the bagels and lox we served, the table was filled with ethnic treats brought over by other parents. In fact, there is hardly an occasion that Mrs. Pethcry doesn't send over some Thai spring rolls with Sara's good friend Melanie because she knows how much we enjoy them.

Could there be a more fitting environment to prepare our youth for the challenges of life in this millennium?

NOTES

1. Sonia Nieto, "What Does It Mean to Affirm Diversity?" *School Administrator* 56, no. 5 (May 1999): 6–7.

2. See *The Impact of Racial and Ethnic Diversity on Educational Outcomes: Cambridge, MA, School District* (Cambridge, Mass.: Civil Rights Project, Harvard University, 2002), and Michael Kurlaender and John T. Yun, "Is Diversity a Compelling Educational Interest? Evidence from Metropolitan Louisville," in *Diversity Challenged*, ed. Gary Orfield (Cambridge, Mass.: Harvard Education Publishing Group, 2001).

12

SOCIETY REALITY 2

Our Nation's School Population Is Becoming More Diverse, but Our Schools Are Becoming More Segregated

> Whites are the only racial group attending schools where the overwhelming majority of students are of their own race. But given the vast racial changes that today's white students will confront in their communities and jobs, a lack of interracial experience in school may well be a handicap.
>
> —Gary Orfield, "Our Resegregated Schools"[1]

When I began researching the underpinnings of the importance of diverse schools to our society, I assumed I would be writing a chapter on the increasing diversity in our schools, reflecting the changing demographics of our nation. After all, our youth will be the most diverse segment of our population. Currently 35 percent of U.S. children are members of minority groups and this is expected to reach more than 50 percent by 2040. But demographic research shows the makeup of our school populations is much more complex.

Yes, the number of minorities among our student populations is increasing, but disturbing research from the Harvard Civil Rights Project shows that our schools are actually becoming more segregated. The most segregated group is white students. "White children, who will increasingly find themselves working as adults in interracial workplaces, are growing up in more segregated schools than any other racial group, even in many places where the minority population has soared and the white population plummeted," the Harvard report states.[2]

There are a number of factors driving this resegregation, but one is the notorious "white flight": white families move out of neighborhoods when minorities move in. Schools with increasing minority populations see fewer white faces. In some white communities where students have the opportunity to attend diverse regional schools, the majority of the middle-class families choose private schools.

Much of the nation's recent demographic shift can be seen in America's traditionally white suburbs. According to well-respected demographer Harold Hodgkinson, the key areas are the suburban rings. The inner ring, just outside the city, saw the first wave of minorities and immigrants filing into their schools over the last decade or two. Now the diversity is increasing in the next ring, another suburb away from the city.[3]

Annandale High School is at the inner cusp of the second suburban ring around Washington, D.C., experiencing the intense wave of demographic change that Hodgkinson describes. I've seen firsthand how a neighborhood with an influx of immigrants begins to lose middle-class families. We've had to continually work at keeping the young middle-class white families in our increasingly diverse school district. We've also had to address the fears of middle-class families from racial and ethnic minorities who seek out predominantly white schools because of the mystique that these schools are better for their kids.

In many cases, the flight outward soon makes little difference. The middle-class families follow the herd pushing farther and farther away from the urban core (with increasing commutes by parents) in search of the untainted white community. In reality, these communities will soon see immigrants and minorities entering the outer suburbs as well. Maybe, just maybe, these parents will get their kids through school before they have to confront all the things they fear about diverse schools. Or maybe they will have to move again, as some do.

Those of us who stay in these diverse school districts don't feel like we're part of some great social experiment, using our kids as guinea pigs. On the contrary, we feel we know some cherished secret that the other families didn't hear. We told them, and we keep trying to tell them, but the din of the myths about diverse schools keeps getting their attention.

They trust the wisdom of those who made the choice to move away, rather than listen to those who know the inside of these schools first-hand, because the misperceptions are so ingrained.

There are families that don't fit the pattern. Some families investigate for themselves, and trust their instincts and their hearts. When Ari Fox's job took his young family to Chicago, the Foxes decided not only to fight the trend to move to the less diverse suburbs, they decided to stay in the public schools of Chicago. They didn't listen to the voices telling them they couldn't find a good public school in Chicago. Instead they checked it out for themselves.

Mollie Fox talked to school officials who run the magnet program for the Chicago schools and asked for suggestions for magnet and neighborhood schools. She talked to a number of principals as well as parents of students who attended the schools. She visited the schools and went to PTA meetings. The Fox's choice was Blaine Elementary. They found a dynamic principal leading a school with a sound curriculum and a creative approach to academics and electives. The Fox family is part of a small, but growing number of middle-class families returning to the public schools, rather than choosing private schools or moving farther away from the city they enjoy.

Whole communities have experienced the benefits of diversity and fought to save it, even as courts have questioned the educational value of different races in the school population. The schools of Cambridge, Massachusetts, have determined that one way to achieve diversity in their school enrollment is to consider the significant factor of family income. Parents are permitted to list schools they would like their children to attend and decisions on placement are based partially on creating a mix of poor and middle-income students in the classroom. Other cities including San Francisco and Charlotte, North Carolina, are also using income, rather than race, to create schools that have a broad mix of students.

Beverly Hills High School in California has students from many ethnicities and races, with about a third of its student body born outside the United States. One of the ways it maintains its range of student perspectives is by enrolling students from the Los Angeles Unified District, one of the few remaining suburban programs to do so. When the Beverly Hills School Board attempted to end that program, the community was up in arms. A leader of the Beverly Hills Chamber of Commerce stated that he benefited from the interaction among students from both areas when he attended Beverly Hills in the '70s, and he wanted his children to have the same advantages. The community won, and the diversity of the school remains intact.

Middle-class parents in Jackson, Mississippi, were frustrated that their schools had become a dual system: underfunded black public schools and largely white elite private academies, which had been formed to circumvent desegregation orders in the early 1970s. By the mid-1980s a number of middle-class parents had had enough. They wanted their children to have the benefits of a public education, which includes attending a diverse school. These parents began recruiting their peers back to the public schools. Within 18 months, a core group of 20 grew to 800 families. They effectively stemmed the tide of middle-class, largely white, families flowing away from the public schools, making these schools an acceptable alternative for any parent.

Seeing the power of involved parents, the Jackson group evolved into a national organization, called Parents for Public Schools (PPS), with the emphasis on supporting parent efforts to play a proactive role in improving schools in their community.[4] "Our philosophy is unique," says PPS President Kelly Butler. "We are working to make schools better by helping parents have a voice that supports all kids. We are helping parents across lines of race, language, ethnicity, and economics." PPS works at the district level, rather than school level, trying to achieve systemic change that improves all schools in the district. "This is not about 'my kids.' This is about all kids. If the schools aren't good for some kids, they aren't good for all kids," says Butler.

Residents of Brandywine School District, a suburban-urban mix including Wilmington, Delaware, have been part of a remarkable cycle in public education. The *Brown v. Board of Education* case began in Wilmington. In the late 1970s, Brandywine was formed in response to one of the most invasive desegregation court orders in the country. In 1994, the mandate for integration was lifted, but the community has vociferously battled to keep their schools diverse.

Brandywine School Board President Nancy Doorey has been an outspoken advocate for maintaining the diversity in the schools. As a parent, she wants her children exposed to a broad mix of people. She has listened to the students themselves. "During conversations at the high school," Doorey says, "students say they would never meet others and learn different points of view. They would not have the advantage to learn to get along and learn to work together. The students feel it prepares them to be more successful in a diverse world."

Although Brandywine fought it from the outset, the Delaware legislature passed the Neighborhood Schools Act, mandating students attend schools near their homes. The Brandywine School Board went directly to its residents, holding a public referendum on the question of whether they wanted to revert to neighborhood boundaries much like they had in the 1950s. The board provided the voters with information showing how a plan based exclusively on neighborhoods would relegate a number of schools to pockets of urban poverty, with serious implications for the children who would have to attend those schools. "We had to take this out to the community," says Doorey. "The average man on the street has to own this. Are we standing by our kids or aren't we? This was the avenue for the whole community to coalesce."

"Many people who were supporting the Neighborhood Schools Act hadn't thought it through and realized the implications," says community leader Lynne Kielhorn. She led an educational campaign to illuminate the realities of the new school boundaries.

> We gave ourselves a name—KIDS (Kids In Diverse Schools) Coalition. We started flooding the newspaper with letters to the editor, distributed flyers door to door, appeared on a local talk show. We supported our position with data showing the negative impacts on students in high-poverty schools. We developed an e-mail list of 200 names. From there our information would fan out to other lists, such as the local YWCA, the local American Association of University Women, and the Metropolitan Wilmington Urban League.

"I want this school system to be the best it can be," says Kielhorn whose oldest child is in first grade. "I live in a neighborhood where most of the families send their kids to private school. I don't want to do that. I want them to have the best academic experience they can have, and I think they should be able to get that in the public school. The public school offers so much more . . . that's the diversity," says Kielhorn. She has resisted listening to the neighborhood tales about the public schools.

"You hear warnings from people and then you go there and find it's wonderful. You wonder where it is coming from. They are simply being said by people who have never experienced these schools."

When required by the new state law to submit a neighborhood schools plan, the Brandywine School District fulfilled the requirements of the law, but it also delivered a compelling document—the Brandywine Plan—that supports its current city/suburb school boundaries. Asserting it was not assigning students based on race, which the legislation prohibited, Brandywine said it concluded "that it is necessary for any plan to guard against the creation of schools with unduly high concentrations of children with certain risk factors," including poverty and special education requirements.

"The entire community came out in droves to support the status quo" at a public hearing, says Eleanor Woodard, another leader of the KIDS Coalition. Students spoke passionately against a neighborhoods-only plan that would separate many of their current classmates into high-poverty urban schools. "How can we create winners and losers among our schools and the students assigned to them?" asked Sharon Greenbaum, a senior at Concord High School. Business leader Beverley Baxter charged the bill was nothing more than "the 'Wilmington Re-segregation Bill. And we don't want it." In a striking victory for the community, the Delaware State Board of Education unanimously approved the Brandywine Plan that would retain its diverse schools.

All parents want what's best for their children. Yet many seem to be overlooking the incredible strengths of diverse schools, strengths that create passionate advocates out of parents and students who attend them. Children learn to think for themselves, develop new and broadening friendships, and are simply better prepared for the future in schools that have students from different backgrounds. In many cases, once parents and students get a taste of true diversity in their schools, they fight to maintain it. Unfortunately, the people on the other side of the fight are often those who build their case on thirdhand information and ungrounded fears. And the parents with young families are caught in the middle as they try to decide which school is best for their children.

A few years ago, I led a meeting in an elementary school library packed with parents who had come to hear firsthand information about Annandale High School. In our effort to debunk the myths, we brought students, parents, and faculty from the high school to give testimony to the positive academic and social environment.

As the meeting opened to questions, a longtime real estate agent from the neighborhood stood up. His own children had attended Annandale High fifteen years earlier when it was virtually all white. He wasn't quite sure how he felt about the changes in the surrounding community that now included an array of immigrants from every continent. "So what you are telling me is that you are taking lemons and making lemonade," he said.

"No," I quickly replied, "we've got the most delicious, exotic fruit salad you can imagine, and I hope every child in this neighborhood is lucky enough to taste it."

NOTES

1. Gary Orfield, "Our Resegregated Schools," *Principal Magazine* 79, no. 5 (May 2000): 6–11.

2. Gary Orfield, *Schools More Separate* (Cambridge, Mass.: Civil Rights Project, Harvard University, 2001), 17.

3. Harold Hodgkinson, "Educational Demographics: What Teachers Should Know," *Educational Leadership* 58, no. 4 (December 2000/January 2001).

4. See www.Parents4PublicSchools.com.

WHAT ABOUT THE
SCHOOLS NEAR ME?

Alone we can do so little. Together we can do so much.

—Helen Keller (from a plaque on the desk of Walnut Hill Elementary School Principal Jo Anne Hughes)

People often say to me, "Annandale High sounds like a great place, but that school near me has lots of problems." My first question is always, "Where did you get your information? Was it from someone who is involved with the school right now?" In almost every case, the person is simply relaying the neighborhood buzz, gleaned from gossip at the playground or from less-than-accurate media accounts.

I'm not discounting that there are lots of diverse schools with lots of problems. But more often than not, these schools also have great strengths that are being overlooked. As I'm describing Annandale High in glowing terms from my personal experience, there are parents in nearby communities casting aspersions on it because of what "they heard about it." I meet them all the time. They are not bad people, just misinformed. Very often, they are open to the facts when they hear them.

I visited an amazing school in Dallas: Walnut Hill Elementary. As soon as I walked into the building I knew I was someplace special. The bright halls were filled with the creative work of the students. In every class-room I passed, the students were actively engaged in learning. Every teacher I spoke with was brimming with positive things to say about the students, as well as their colleagues and the principal. The classroom where "gifted and talented" students received enrichment included children of every race in the school. The teachers enthusiastically spoke of the many collaborative projects involving faculty and students across grades, including new English learners and special education students. Principal Jo Anne Hughes's office was not only packed with student work, but plaques recognizing the many teachers who have won awards, the national and state honors for the school, and her own recognition as Dallas Principal of the Year. Yet as Hughes and I discussed the innovative approaches to learning throughout the building, we also talked of the many middle-class parents near the school who chose to send their children to private school. I cannot believe that any one of those parents ever stepped foot in the school because once there, every myth they believed about this diverse school would evaporate. Many terrific schools around the country fight this battle every day. "If we could just get the parents in the door . . ." I hear over and over.

There is a quirky radio ad for the Baltimore Opera that ends with, "Opera—it's better than you think. . . . It has to be." That goes for diverse schools, as well. Those of us with a personal connection to these schools know if we can get parents and students to take an honest look at them, their eyes will open to new insights. While Annandale High loses some students from families who move before high school or send their children to private schools, we rarely lose students once they begin as freshman. The loyalty is dramatic.

Liz Segall has been on both sides of the coin. She says:

> When my oldest daughter approached high school age, I became nervous, not about the diversity at Annandale High, but about the educational opportunities that she would have. I just wasn't confident that enough would be demanded of her in a school where there were so many different kinds of kids, and where more than a third of the kids were in families with income levels so low that they were eligible for free or reduced price lunches. We made the decision to send her to a private school her freshman year—smaller classes, tougher courses. By the end of that year we knew that she had been academically challenged, but we were not happy

with other things at the school. Some of the classes she really wanted to take, in particular photography, were canceled due to lack of interest. We discovered there just were not enough kids in the school to fill all the classes that were advertised in the glossy brochure.

Segall was particularly concerned that daughter Laura's social expectations changed from when she was part of a diverse middle school. "When she asked us why we didn't go skiing in Aspen over spring break, I knew this had been a wrong turn for us," Segall says.

The Segalls began doing some firsthand investigating of their neighborhood high school. "That spring Laura spent the day at Annandale High with a friend and we spent a couple hours with the guidance counselor talking about course choices. The next year she entered Annandale as a happy sophomore who had an elective in photography. Once I realized that her courses were academically challenging and that she had adjusted well, I felt back on track." Laura went on to study photography at the Rochester Institute of Technology and is now a photojournalist.

A few years later, Segall became the president of the PTA at Annandale High when her third daughter entered the school. "What I have discovered talking to other parents is that those like me, who were at one time so filled with doubt and fear, often become the most passionate advocates for the school," Segall says. "Maybe it is because we have really examined our choices, and we chose a diverse school. Maybe it is because we felt as if we were misled by 'knowledge' that is common, but wrong."

Gladys Vaccarezza of Blaine Elementary School in Chicago has succeeded in getting middle-class parents to take a look at her school, turning around community support in the decade she has been principal. Her diverse neighborhood ranges from a battered woman's shelter and apartments to expensive condominiums and new homes. She has instituted a number of initiatives to strengthen the academics of the school, including a fine arts magnet program that crosses the curriculum. And, she has concentrated on improving relations with the neighborhood. In Chicago, parents can apply to send their children to any magnet school or school with a magnet program; popular schools fill up fast. Blaine has become so popular in its own neighborhood as well as among other parents, that it drew 245 applicants for 35 available slots in kindergarten in 2002. Nearly seventy kindergarteners stayed on from the popular preschool, which draws largely from the neighborhood. Vaccarezza believes a school is stronger if its enrollment is predominantly from its own neighborhood, because it is easier for families to be connected to the school.

She says the first thing she had to do to win over the neighborhood was to change the school's physical image. Few people realized the building, erected in 1893, was a school. "We replaced windows and created a campus feeling outside and did a variety of things to get people to notice it was a school," she says. "We changed the interior as well, displaying students' work throughout the building."

Then, Vaccarezza had to draw neighborhood parents inside. She recruited teacher and parent volunteers to give tours of the building every Wednesday morning. After the tour, she sits down with the group to answer any questions. The tours are advertised on a marquee outside the school. "These tours are very popular," Vaccarezza says. "Parents come up to me and tell me this is their second or third tour, and they brought their neighbor this time. I love to see this," Vaccarezza says. She recalls one woman from one of the newer homes nearby who came over to put her child on a list for future enrollment. When Vaccarezza asked her how old her child was, the woman pointed to her overstretched maternity top.

"Once the parents come into the building, they see the school with different eyes," says Vaccarezza. Some parents from other neighborhoods come on the tour, complaining about what they have heard about their own school. "I tell them to give the other school a chance," Vaccarezza says. "You never know what's going on until you go inside. You've got to feel it. I tell them to bring their children. They will tell you whether this is the right place or not."

As with all diverse schools, Vaccarezza gets lots of questions about test scores. "I tell them that test scores are only one indicator of what happened on one day, not what is going on in an entire school. That is why you have to 'feel' the school. Go and visit and see if this is your school. Is this the safe and nurturing place you want for your child?"

No school is a perfect place. Each one is unique with its own strengths and weaknesses. While diverse schools have so much to offer, they have many challenges that must be faced. Some need our attention more than others do. It's become a cliché, but it truly does "take a village" to help a diverse school be all that it should be. There is an im-

portant role for everyone in the community—school boards, superintendents, principals, teachers, students, parents, and community members. When we all do our part, the pieces of the whole come together
like a prism that captures and then releases a rainbow before your eyes.

So what can you do to help make these schools the extraordinary
places they can be? I was hoping you'd ask. Part 3 provides strategies for
each of us—educators, parents, and ordinary citizens—who have a stake
in strengthening diverse schools.

III

HOW TO REAP THE RICH HARVEST OF OUR DIVERSE SCHOOLS

"Jazz Club," by Julia Ehrenfeld

14

WHAT'S MY ROLE?

School leaders from every level are key to shaping school culture. Principals communicate core values in their everyday work. Teachers reinforce values in their actions and words. Parents bolster spirit when they visit school, participate in governance, and celebrate successes. In the strongest schools, leadership comes from many sources.

—Kent D. Peterson and Terrence E. Deal, "How Leaders Influence the Culture of Schools"[1]

This book is based on several key premises. The first is that schools with a mixture of races and ethnic groups provide unique academic and social opportunities for all students, the faculty, and the entire community. The second premise is that these benefits flow only if the school has strong leadership actively pursuing academic excellence for all students, providing equity of opportunity, and promoting respect of each individual's background and perspective.

The third premise is equally important. For a diverse school to be well run, it must have the active support of the entire school community. Diverse schools provide so many opportunities for enlightenment, enrichment, and enjoyment. But they present tough challenges that must be taken on with vigor and optimism, not just by the principal and a few

classroom teachers, but by everyone who has a stake in that school succeeding, which is the entire community.

There is a mind-set that is palpable in a community where a diverse
school is thriving. There is a clear sense of commitment to *every* child, not
just the children who succeed easily, or the ones who star on the football
field, or the students with the engaging smile, or even the ones who help
out their fellow students. There's a commitment to finding the key to
reaching the students who sit too quietly in the back of the room or the
ones who never seem to get the assignment right or the ones who miss
school too often. There is a commitment to helping all students learn by
involving whole families, breaking down barriers that make it more difficult for some parents to be involved in their children's education. And
there is a commitment to building a unified community where everyone—
adults as well as youth—respects and learns from one another.

These successful schools have moved beyond the finger-pointing that
still exists in some schools. It's always easy to blame the victims. You'll
hear some principals and teachers bemoan the fact that the same methods they've been using for decades aren't as effective today, and there-
fore it must be the students and parents who are failing the schools. In
truth, the schools are failing those families when they use teaching
strategies designed for homogeneous classrooms, and set a tone that
values the dominant white culture alone.

One parent leader told me about two high schools in her school district with nearly identical diverse demographics. One school was thriving, with student achievement high for all students, and a building
filled with animated students who mix across cultures during class and
afterward. In the other school, an institutional ethos prevailed where
only certain students were expected to succeed. Students lived up to
those lowered expectations and the lowered opportunities that natu-
rally followed—there was a much higher dropout rate in the second
school, particularly for African American males. You could feel the difference in the two cultures just walking in the halls.

Libia Gil, superintendent of Chula Vista Elementary School District
in San Diego County, says that school leaders—including principals,
teachers, and parents—need to operate in a culture that keeps a focus
on serving the needs of students, not on meeting adult needs. Gil describes the approach this way:

[One] leadership tool is understanding the choice to operate either in the "Blame Frame" or the "Aim Frame." The two basic questions posed in the Blame Frame are:

- What is wrong?
- Who is to blame?

The Blame Frame has the effect of shifting responsibility to others. In contrast, the two basic questions that characterized the Aim Frame are:

- What is the goal?
- How can we get there?[2]

In a well-run diverse school, there is recognition that everyone has a role to play, and that these responsibilities are different than they would be in a homogeneous school.

Complacency doesn't cut it. There is a constant need to observe, analyze, and develop strategies that will enable every child to achieve at his or her potential. There is a strong belief that the school is there to serve the needs of all children, not a select few, and certainly not to meet the needs of adults. This applies to school boards, superintendents, principals, and teachers, but it also carries over to parents, students themselves, and community members.

Part 3 outlines strategies for each local group with a responsibility for assuring that diverse schools fulfill their promise. In many communities, all the parts of the whole come together in a powerful academic institution that becomes the focal point of the community. Because I come from a family where music has great meaning, when I see a vibrant school community, I often think of an orchestra with a strong, enthusiastic conductor and competent artists playing their parts with commitment. Each musician takes individual responsibility to play the part well, to support and complement the other parts, combining into a glorious whole. Everyone in the audience, as well as the orchestra itself, is part of one grand tour de force.

It's time for all of us to tune our instruments.

NOTES

1. Kent D. Peterson and Terrence E. Deal, "How Leaders Influence the Culture of Schools," *Educational Learership* 56, no. 1 (September 1998): 28.

2. Libia Gil and Dennis M. Doyle, "A District Responds: Embracing Diversity," *State Education Standard* (Winter 2002): 20–25.

⑮

SCHOOL BOARDS:
LEADING THEIR COMMUNITY

Regardless of their race, ethnicity or gender, school board members and administrators are charged with educating a student body that is more diverse than any generation before them. Their challenge, amid teacher shortages, shrinking budgets, and overcrowded classrooms, is to make sure the children of today's generation are just as prepared as previous generations to achieve the American Dream.

—Kathleen Vail, "The Changing Face of Education"[1]

The school board is the most direct link between members of the community and their educational system. You don't get to vote for a principal, but you do get to vote for your school board in most communities. And it is not just parents who have the opportunity to vote, but every eligible voter. The school board best serves the voters by establishing meaningful policies that result in strong well-run schools, the linchpin of a good community.

Some school boards are mired in petty politics and power struggles with the superintendent. Issues such as phonics and math drills become political rallying cries, rather than instructional strategies that must be carefully considered as part of comprehensive approaches. The needs of students become secondary to the agenda of individual board members.

Other school boards are shining examples of leadership. They tackle problems thoughtfully, evaluating research, reviewing data, and carefully considering the needs of their students. Debate is vigorous, but the unified goal of supporting the education of every child carries the day.

While the school board does represent the community, in diverse communities it rarely *reflects* the community. As diversity is climbing in many of our nation's schools, school boards still are largely composed of white males. Eighty-six percent of board members are white, according to a 2001 survey conducted for the National School Boards Association (NSBA). More than 60 percent of school board members are male, even though the vast majority of educators are female, and far more mothers than fathers are active in schools nationwide.[2]

This makes it more difficult, but certainly not impossible, for school boards to understand and support diverse student bodies. School boards must make serious efforts to reach out to their diverse communities and gain a depth of understanding of the strengths the minorities bring to the school system and the obstacles they face in taking advantage of the educational opportunities. Many school boards have accepted the challenge and shown extraordinary leadership in this arena, not only improving the life of students in that community but improving the lives of all the residents.

School boards can show leadership in supporting diverse schools in a number of ways:

Set school policies that are sensitive to cultural differences without harming individuals' rights.

School boards can be sensitive to the rights of minority students in ways that do not infringe on the rights of other students. For example, students who wish to cover their heads for religious reasons, such as Sikh boys or Muslim girls or Orthodox Jews, can be permitted to do so even if the school prohibits hats. Some schools do a much better job of this than others. Clear guidance from the school board is the way to ensure consistent policies from school to school in that district.

School calendars should cause the least potential disruption to families trying to celebrate religious holidays. In Fairfax County, the spring vacation week usually includes both Christian Easter and Jewish Passover, when possible. One year, the first day of school was set for Rosh

Hashanah, the Jewish New Year, one of the holiest days of the Jewish calendar. While Jewish students were used to missing school for their holidays, being forced to be absent on the first day of school was an extraordinary hardship. Our own rabbi's daughter was about to start high school that year, a difficult transition in itself. The Jewish community was able to gain the understanding of the school board that starting a day later would have no detrimental effect on most students and teachers, but it would be tremendously beneficial for Jewish students and faculty. School began one day later than originally planned. Years later, the vast majority of parents in Fairfax County don't remember the day school started that year, but every Jewish parent remembers it clearly.

Provide the resources needed to meet the special challenges of diverse schools.

Yes, students with different ethnic and racial backgrounds add a great deal to the school community, but they also bring many special needs with them. Schools for the most part have been created to meet the needs of the dominant white culture. When other groups enter the mix, extra resources are required. Sometimes these are specific to the group, such as classes to teach English to those who speak other languages. Sometimes, however, these extra resources are spent on programs that benefit the entire school, such as schoolwide initiatives at the elementary level to raise reading comprehension, or in-school SAT preparation.

Many of these programs require significant resources to make them effective. School boards need to wrestle with the same issues with which we as a nation at large wrestle—how to provide needed services with limited budgets. But they must constantly look at the programs that are making a difference with diverse populations and place a high priority on those. Successful diverse schools have the resources that provide the means to help every child to succeed.

Make structural changes that will enhance diversity, such as drawing school attendance boundaries to create more diverse school populations.

Schools in individual neighborhoods seem like a good idea. But one neighborhood school may lose enrollment as the age of nearby homeowners rises, while other nearby neighborhoods are bursting with young children from new homes and apartments. Many school boards must deal with the issue of equalizing population among their district schools. That gives them the opportunity to look carefully at more than just student numbers to try to create a balance among races, ethnicities, and socioeconomic groups. According to the NSBA, race and ethnicities can be used as one factor in devising school boundaries. "Courts as high as the Supreme Court have respected the rights of local school boards to make decisions that are right for that community," says Edwin Darden, NSBA's senior staff attorney. He notes that courts have recognized the benefits of a diverse student population, and also that the issues at the K–12 level are different than they are in the workplace or even in higher education. Notwithstanding other legal requirements governing their district, a school board basically may draw boundaries that maximize a diversity in the populations, but it must show that the boundaries are drawn in a practical way, that there is a "compelling interest" that justifies the boundaries, and that the boundaries are narrowly drawn to meet that interest. While different courts have set the bar for meeting these requirements at different heights, school boards around the country are succeeding at drawing school boundaries that maximize the benefits of diversity.[3] Some school districts, such as San Francisco and Cambridge, Massachusetts, have avoided race as an issue, striving to create balance in their schools by using socioeconomic status, which is often related to race and ethnicity as well.

Some school boards have shown great leadership in creating and maintaining boundaries that result in diverse schools. It was the school board in the Brandywine School District in Delaware that led the courageous and successful battle to keep its schools diverse. The board's actions displayed competence, caring, and political savvy. The board worked within the mandate created by new state legislation to develop a plan for all students to attend "neighborhood schools." At the same time, however, the board held a referendum on whether the Brandywine community wanted to change the existing school boundaries that had created schools with a diverse mix of students from the city of Wilmington and the nearby suburbs. The vote was overwhelmingly in favor of the status quo, including strong support from students, parents, the business community, and senior citizens, "If the intent of the law is to honor the wishes of the community, then the community has spoken," says Nancy Doorey, president of the Brandywine School Board. So the board submitted not only the required plan for new boundaries, but also a plan to maintain the status quo that provided convincing arguments on how the new boundaries would cause serious harm to some students. Picking up on the legislation's language that the school boundaries should be "fair and equitable" to all children, the board effectively argued in its submission to the state that returning to schools based only on neighborhood boundaries would create schools locked in poverty, with all the inequities that follow. Supporting the extraordinary work of the Brandywine School Board, the Delaware Board of Education unanimously approved its recommendation to maintain the current boundaries.

Support programs that reach out to parents and community members of different races and ethnic backgrounds.

School boards can be at the forefront of efforts to build cohesive communities out of diverse population groups. The school board in Storm Lake, Iowa, played a key role in helping the community adjust to a wave of immigration in the '80s and '90s that changed the population from largely middle-class white to nearly half minorities. Jan Patton, a longtime Storm Lake resident and landlord has also been a member of the school board for nearly ten years. She said that the board learned through a community survey that prejudice was prevalent in the existing community. The Storm Lake School Board knew it needed to find ways to bring the community together. Patton credits the earliest acceptance of the new immigrants to a community education program in the early 1990s called "Rockin' Readers" in which older white residents went into classrooms to read to students. Many of the students, mostly from Laos and Cambodia at that time, could not read English, but they could understand what was being read to them. It was in the classroom, with one-on-one connections, that the attitudes began to change. She watched residents whom she described as "white-minded" become completely enamored with the young children they met.

The Storm Lake School Board took pains to make minority parents feel welcome. It began advertising public board meetings in flyers that were translated in Spanish, Laotian, and Vietnamese, and on public service announcements in native languages on the local radio station. Patton would regularly visit families in the rental properties she owned, providing them access to a familiar and friendly school board member.

To ease the language barrier, she joked about the fledgling Spanish she had learned through a few classes.

Patton says that every member of the school board was committed to helping the recent immigrants become a part of the broader community. Board members became outspoken champions of the benefits of diversity. "Whenever we had a chance to speak of diversity in other towns or at state conventions, we used positive terms," Patton said.

The educational leaders in Storm Lake, including the school board and school-based leaders, truly accepted the mantle of leadership and became a beacon of light for the entire community. According to Public Safety Director Mark Prosser, "Our schools have been a leader and a driving force in our community." Prosser, who is chief of police and administrative leader of the fire department, believes that all the students in Storm Lake are benefiting from the strengths of its diverse schools. "Ten years ago, our kids didn't really understand that there is more to the world than just white people. Today our students better appreciate and understand what the world is all about."

Encourage programs such as peer mediation that teach students of different cultures how to work out disagreements in a nonviolent way.

We need to teach our students ways to handle the disagreements that will inevitably arise. Yes, it is important to send a message that violent behavior will not be tolerated in any form. However, to suspend students for fighting without finding the root cause and without teaching them how to handle conflict in a nonviolent way will only lead to more and bigger conflicts. Annandale High School's peer mediation program, which has been nationally recognized, has shown students from every country in the world that conflicts can be handled without violence. A key element of the success of the program is that student peer mediators at Annandale are leaders in the school who are treated with respect by everyone from the principal to fellow students. They are not necessarily the top academic achievers or the luminaries in extracurricular activities. In fact, they are often recruited from among the "regular kids" or those who have been through difficult personal times themselves. There is an emphasis on finding peer mediators from among the many ethnic groups in the school. The qualities they all possess are a caring attitude and an ability to truly listen to what others say. And for these important qualities, and the essential work they do, they are valued and shown great respect within the school.

There are a host of other important programs that help create a school culture of respect, such as character education initiatives. At Walnut Hill Elementary in Dallas, the entire school is involved in a character education activity every third week. Under Success Through Accepting Responsibility (STARS) all 450 students in grades K–6 are divided into mixed-grade teams of 10 students. Each team is assigned to a caring adult, with every member of the faculty and staff involved except for the counselor, principal, and secretary. The group then works together on a character-building project. The faculty member remains with the same team year to year, with sixth graders graduating and new kindergarteners joining the group. The program forges important relationships between adults and students as well as among the students themselves. "The fun part is watching the older kids taking the younger kids hands and walking them back to class. This is a real sign character education is having an impact," says principal Jo Anne Hughes.

These programs are most effective when there is a coordination from elementary through middle and high school. The key is to be proactive and make a long-term commitment to programs that will make a difference.

Choose instructional materials that represent a variety of cultures.

Every teacher will tell you that students learn better when they are engaged in the instruction. It is hard to be engaged when all the textbooks and additional materials represent a culture that is not your own. It is important for racial and ethnic minority students to see people like themselves represented in positive ways in curriculum materials. This gives the materials a relevance to their lives and takes on an authenticity that materials featuring only white culture cannot.

It is truly important for every student to see a variety of cultures represented in materials. It is a critical part of building a community based on interest in and respect for other religions, cultures, and nationalities. And it is a significant part of the education of students who will meet people of many different backgrounds in the workforce of the future.[4]

School board members can be the leaders of not only the schools but the entire community, helping to bring all the diverse elements together. Or they can stick their heads in the sand and spend more time on micromanaging the school system and wrangling with the superintendent. It's a tough job either way, but courageous in only one way.

NOTES

1. Kathleen Vail, "The Changing Face of Education," *Education Vital Signs*, supplement to the *American School Board Journal* 188, no. 12 (December 2001).

2. Kathleen Vail, "The Changing Face of Education."

3. For guidance on the legal requirements, see Edwin C. Darden, Arthur L. Coleman, and Scott R. Palmer, *From Desegregation to Diversity: A School District's Self-Assessment Guide on Race, Student Assignment and the Law* (Washington, D.C.: National School Boards Association, 2002), available through the association's website, www.nsba.org.

4. See James A. Banks and Cherry A. McGee, *The Handbook of Research on Multicultural Education* (New York: Jossey-Bass, 2001).

16

SUPERINTENDENTS: VISIONARIES WITH A COLLABORATIVE SPIRIT

> While the job [of superintendent] is fraught with external pressures, it is filled with internal possibilities. Superintendents know they can change the trajectory of children's lives, alter the behavior of organizations, and expand the possibilities of whole communities. . . . As education stands in the national spotlight, there are few roles as complex or as pivotal as that of the public school superintendent.
>
> —Paul Houston, "Superintendents for the 21st Century: It's Not Just a Job, It's a Calling"[1]

Superintendents are the visionaries of the school community. They articulate the goals of the system and motivate their administrators to meet those goals. Good superintendents clearly lay out expectations for their principals, delegate the responsibility for running the schools to them, and hold them accountable for the results. When all is said and done, however, it is the superintendent who will answer for what happens in the school system—from whether the buses are safe to whether the students are learning to read to whether parents feel welcome in the schools. Effective superintendents celebrate the successes of the school district, sharing the recognition and praise, and lead efforts to make necessary improvements.

A superintendent must be a team player. With the school board on one side, developing policies and providing resources (as well as hiring and firing the superintendent), and the principals on the other side, running the schools on a day-to-day basis, the superintendent must be gifted at collaboration. Beyond the school district itself, effective superintendents build coalitions, marshaling the resources of parents and other residents, business leaders, foundations, and any other sources of assistance. Effective superintendents are also politically savvy, able to gain the respect of government officials as well as local and state legislators.

While they are charged with collaborating with all the social and political forces of the community, superintendents are also expected to be strong leaders, willing to take courageous actions. "You have to be willing to risk everything to be a successful superintendent," says Estanislado (Stan) Paz who leads the Tucson Unified School District. "You have to be willing to play all out so you are free to make the right decisions and right recommendations. Sometimes if you have to hold back on doing what you think is right for personal reasons—economic gain, stability, ego—you will face your biggest barrier in being effective in your role."

In the ideal world, superintendents in this country would be from a diversity of backgrounds. However a striking 95 percent of superintendents are white and 87 percent are male. That's truly a shame. I live in a district with one of only a few dozen Hispanic superintendents. He understands what it is like to come to a country not speaking the language of the teacher or the grocery store clerk. He knows what it feels like to sit in the back of the room, quiet, hoping not to be noticed, when you desperately need the teacher's attention. He knows the striving of immigrant parents who come here seeking the best for their families, including the best education for their children. And today, he knows what a powerful role model he can be to all students, no matter what their background.

Dan Domenech of Fairfax County, Virginia, who came to this country from Cuba as a child, knows there is more to being a superintendent than how students are taught. "Running the school system is not just an issue of pedagogy—why we teach what we teach," Domenech says. "There are issues of emotion, bias, racism, and politics involved. The key issue is balancing the pedagogy that is appropriate against the political and social issues," he says.

Many other superintendents who did not have the advantage of growing up as a member of a minority group do develop a keen sensitivity to the needs of diverse populations. Superintendents around the country take on the seemingly impossible job of running entire school systems, often composed of schools of varying populations and needs, trying to provide a sound education for all the students no matter what strengths and weaknesses they bring to school.

Superintendents can build the diverse schools in their district in a number of ways:

Look beyond standardized test scores to measure the success of a school.

Standardized tests provide valuable information, but as pointed out in chapter 1, they should not be the only measure of a school's worth. Superintendents should consider a wide range of factors in measuring the success of schools and their leadership:

- What is the tone of the school? (Do groups coexist in tension or have the students become one community celebrating its diversity? Are students encouraged to share their own unique backgrounds and experiences or are they required to check their heritage at the door?)
- Do administrators and teachers have high expectations for all students? (Does the curriculum provide challenge for all students? Are there targeted initiatives aimed at reducing barriers to achievement? Are minority students well represented in enrichment activities and rigorous classes?)
- Are teachers partners in the school's progress? (Do teachers collaborate across grades and across the curriculum? Are they given the opportunity to take part in relevant professional development opportunities? Are teachers part of collaborative decision-making bodies both at the school level and districtwide?)
- Do the students and teachers have the resources they need? (Does the principal make wise decisions on using available resources within the context of the needs of that community? Are parents and community members motivated to donate time and materials; and are these utilized in a coherent way that meets the goals of the school?)

- Is the school a focal point of the neighborhood? (Do parents and community members feel welcome in the school? Does the principal use creative outreach strategies to reach parents of diverse backgrounds? Does the school have vibrant partnerships with community and business organizations?)

Speak out on the strengths of diversity, not just the challenges to be overcome.

The superintendent is the voice of the school system in the greater community. The very words used by the superintendent to describe diverse schools can have tremendous impact on the way these schools are viewed. A superintendent who passionately champions the value of diverse education can open the eyes of a chamber of commerce member who has no children, or a civic association leader whose children graduated years ago, or a young parent trying to decide where to move her family. Mary Barter, superintendent in Durango, Colorado, feels it is important for the community to understand that the schools must teach students to respect other individuals, no matter how they differ. A diverse school is "a rich experience for students, and for staff members and their families," Barter states. "School is a preparation for life. What kind of preparation is a school that doesn't resemble real life at all?"

Joe Cirasuolo, superintendent of schools in Wallingford, Connecticut, believes it is part of his job to articulate the values of diversity to the community at large. "You have to be patient and persistent," he says. "Look for one opportunity after another." He seeks ways for the students from his predominantly white district to be exposed to students from diverse backgrounds. One opportunity is Project Choice, a program that enables students from New Haven to attend school in the nearby suburbs. Cirasuolo declares as many slots as possible open in every school for the students from the city. Supporting diversity "is more than good, it's vital. Every interaction helps us grow and become better human beings," he says.

Analyze the unique needs of diverse schools and provide them with the support needed to address these needs.

Many districts comprise schools of differing populations and needs. It is the superintendent's job to make sure each school is taking the appropriate steps to meet those needs and is provided with the necessary resources. "We take the philosophy that we change one building at a time," says Vic Meyers, superintendent in Harrison District No. 2 in Colorado Springs, Colorado. "We've done extensive research on programs that close the gap for student achievement for underachieving groups. We allow each school to select the model they wish to apply in that building," he says. Administrators and faculty in the twenty-one-school district visit other schools to see the initiatives firsthand, and they sometimes bring in speakers to address the faculty about the program under consideration. Meyers believes that having the staff involved in researching, selecting, and implementing the program increases faculty buy-in and commitment to making it work.

Superintendent Libia Gil of Chula Vista Elementary School District, the largest kindergarten through sixth grade district in California, takes a similar decentralized approach to school reform. "The goals for students in Chula Vista are nonnegotiable: rigorous standards, high expectations for all our students. But our approach to accomplishing the goals is highly flexible. We have just about every comprehensive reform model in place in different sites in our district," Gil says, describing the host of programs, including five charter schools, in her nearly forty elementary schools. "We place a strong belief in the professionalism of our school-site staff. Working together with appropriate support and data, the school-based leaders are in the best position to make decisions. If they believe the program will be successful, they will make it successful," Gil says.

"While we have a high level of autonomy and responsibility at our sites, the accountability is centralized," Gil says. "We are not particular about the program model if we see a positive impact on student achievement."

Dan Domenech knows that some of the 200-plus schools in Fairfax County have greater needs than others:

> We need to overcome the bias that putting extra resources in the hands of certain schools is unfair to students in other schools. We've made great strides in meeting the needs of special education students, who are often middle class. We need to be willing to put extra resources in schools to help language-minority and students from low socioeconomic back-

grounds, students who don't have parents with the political clout who know how to work the system.

He has instituted a variety of initiatives for schools with high poverty and high minorities, including Project Excel, which puts extra resources in these schools, and year-round calendars in several schools.

Hire administrators who view diversity as a strength.

The strength of a school system is in its building leaders. The principals must share the vision and commitment of the superintendent. It's critical to look for administrators who understand the needs of diverse students and seek ways to reach them. If a principal believes his job is simply managing the resources of the school, he will quickly run up against insurmountable problems. But if the principal believes that his role is to serve the needs of all children, no matter what it takes, that principal will find a way to make it happen. Truly the superintendent will have the partner she needs to make the schools an extraordinary learning environment. "We look for the passion and the advocacy of children when we interview candidates for principal," says Chula Vista's Libia Gil.

Vic Meyers says that the Harrison District works hard at attracting and retaining a diverse staff by modeling a respectful workplace and through extensive recruitment and training. They identify teachers in training from nearby universities who come from a variety of ethnic and racial backgrounds. The district has a "grow your own" program that provides stipends to staff who want to advance in the system. But, as in most school districts, the diversity in the staff still doesn't match the diversity in the student population. "We are constantly working on this goal," says Meyers.

Tucson's Stan Paz has started an aspiring leadership academy to help identify and train a pool of eligible administrators with the skills needed by today's leaders. Administrators are chosen through a rigorous selection process. Paz looks for candidates who can access and analyze data about student achievement, make decisions for school improvement based on that data, and communicate those decisions clearly both in writing and orally. Paz seeks principals who truly believe in the promise of diverse schools. "Some principals had the attitude they could 'put in their time' at a diverse school and transfer to another school. That's no longer acceptable," Paz says. "We want leaders who are committed to making diverse schools the best they can be."

Effective superintendents will always have their eyes open for new leaders, grooming people who have the right attitudes and skills. A superintendent from Ohio who was surveyed for a Public Agenda study on school leadership states, "You have to go after people. The skill of a good superintendent is to identify people. As you see people at meetings, you see them working on different things, you start to build a little file folder on that person in your head."[2]

Paul Houston, who was a superintendent for seventeen years in three states before he became the executive director of the American Association of School Administrators, wrote about the challenges of finding the next generation of administrators, stating,

> The current pipeline into school administration is inverted. There are many people in it who have great potential for leadership. They must be nurtured and encouraged. But the profession can no longer depend solely on those who choose it—i.e., the "wannabes." We must begin to identify a new cadre of leaders who see the role as one of collaboration, rather than of command, and then mentor them into the jobs. These are the "oughtabes," and they must be identified and encouraged.[3]

Provide integrated professional development opportunities.

All faculty need professional development to grow and serve their students better, but those in diverse schools have particular needs. Superintendents must ensure that the district offers a coordinated set of training opportunities, based on the latest research, that provides faculty with the knowledge and skills they need.

Administrators, first and foremost, need opportunities to rejuvenate themselves and keep up with the demands of their job. Principals can feel isolated in their own buildings, carrying the burdens of ensuring the success of their own student body. They need training to augment their skills and expertise, and networking opportunities to exchange ideas and strategies with their peers, particularly those facing similar challenges in diverse schools.

Teachers need extensive opportunities to overcome the barriers set up by our educational system that separates teachers by room and grade. Not only should professional development opportunities be available to teachers, but teachers must be encouraged to take advantage of them. Schoolwide in-service training tailored to the needs of that faculty should be part of the year's calendar. It is important for the entire faculty to explore their own attitudes and beliefs about race and culture because that shapes how they interact with students every day. They must also have opportunities to gain insight into successful strategies for reaching diverse students and their families, including knowledge on the specific needs and challenges of students learning English as a new language. Faculties should also be encouraged to break out of the confines of grade and specialty to collaborate as teams toward the goal of high achievement for all students.

The Mesa Public School District in Arizona offers a comprehensive program of professional development opportunities, including courses and training manuals on working with the diverse populations of the district. Workshops cover issues such as "Unlearning Racism," "Valuing and Managing Diversity," "Counselors and Teachers Developing Cultural Sensitivity in a Pluralistic Society," and "American Indians: The Role and Responsibility of the U.S. Educational System."

The district responds to specific needs as they develop. For a workshop on the Muslim faith, Mesa's diversity specialist Cliff Moon coordinated with the Islamic speaker's bureau in Scottsdale to present a program on "Teaching and Counseling Muslim Students in the School." Teachers learned the principles of the religion and ways to accommodate the special sensitivities of Muslim students, such as girls who could not swim during P.E. in the same area as boys. Teachers have been so interested in this topic that some have done additional work in their own schools. One teacher who took part in an earlier workshop arranged for a speaker at her own school and then coordinated a trip to a mosque.

The Mesa Public School District also addresses diversity issues with the students. Among the programs is one provided to every seventh grade student during geography class. The topics covered by this interactive initiative spell out its title, Project Diversity. These topics include: Diversity awareness, Inclusion, Valuing diversity, Equity issues, Respect for differences, School climate, Interpersonal relationships, Tolerance, and You can make a difference. "We're committed to helping students understand and appreciate their own heritage, as well as other cultural, social and ethnic groups," Moon says.

Fairfax County Public Schools held a "Reach to Teach" conference a few days before school opened, attended by teams from every one of its 132 elementary schools. The conference was designed to help teachers differentiate their instruction to meet the needs of the many different types of learners in their classrooms. It provided the teachers with insights into identifying individual student strengths and varying instruction so that all students can succeed. Demonstrating its commitment to this principle, Fairfax County provided every elementary classroom and resource teacher in the county system with a briefcase packed with resources. The specially developed materials focus on differentiating instruction in the four core academic areas—language arts, mathematics, social studies, and science. The resource books include sidebars with strategies for reaching special groups, such as those with limited English skills, gifted students, and special education students. Each of the school teams went back to their own schools and introduced the resource materials to the rest of their staff, with the help of a training video.[4]

Marshal the resources of the community.

An effective superintendent has one foot in the community and beyond, promoting education and looking for resources that will improve the education of children in that district. Today's students require more than just academic instruction during the school day. To truly learn at their capacity, they must be healthy and secure, with parents who are involved their education. The school system can't support the students alone. It must bring together the resources available beyond the school walls and make the schools a focal point of the community. This strengthens not just the school and its students, but the entire community.

Stan Paz of Tucson brings in business leaders as active partners in developing strategies that will improve the system of 64,000 students. "That is the only way it will work in a community as diverse as ours," Paz says. A blue-ribbon committee of business leaders is reviewing ways for the school system to be run more effectively and efficiently, providing crucial advice in times of dwindling resources.

Marty Blank, staff director of the Coalition for Community Schools, supports schools in their efforts to bring community resources into schools. "In every setting it is important to look at the characteristics and conditions of the children and the families—their assets, problems, cultures—and develop a strategy and specific activities that work best in that setting." Many superintendents find this "community schools" approach an effective way to support and supplement the core instruction in the school by providing services and opportunities that meet the extended needs of students, their families, and the entire community.[5]

Superintendent Mark McNeill of Nanuet School District in Rockland County, New York, is a strong believer in broadening the role of schools in the community. McNeill is a proactive leader who is taking steps to strengthen his entire community, currently with a minority population of about 30 percent. Both the elementary schools and the middle school in the district have Family Resource Centers, based on the School of the 21st Century Concept developed at Yale University, which is a collaborative partner with Nanuet. The centers provide wide-ranging programs including a lending library for parents and children, information and referral services, preschool activities, free parenting workshops and support groups, before- and after-school programs, enrichment classes, and a student mentoring program.

The superintendent's job is not for the faint of heart. A superintendent must be a true leader, sometimes taking controversial steps for the benefit of all students. To rally the followers necessary to turn the broad goals into tangible results, the superintendent also must be a gifted collaborator able to engage all those who care about public education.

NOTES

1. Paul Houston, "Superintendent for the 21st Century: It's Not Just a Job, It's a Calling," *Kappan Magazine* 82, no. 6 (February 2001): 428–33.

2. Steve Farkas, Jean Johnson, Ann Duffett, and Tony Foleno, *Trying to Stay Ahead of the Game* (Washington, D.C.: Public Agenda, 2001), 29.

3. Paul Houston, "Superintendents for the 21st Century."

4. Manuals from the "Reach to Teach" conference are available from Fairfax County Public Schools, www.fcps.edu/DIS/publications.

5. For more information, see www.CommunitySchools.org.

PRINCIPALS: DOING WHATEVER IT TAKES

I've never seen a quality school that didn't have a quality principal.

—Richard Riley, "The 21st Century Principal: Opportunities and Challenges"[1]

The principal is the building leader. If there is one person who can make or break a school, it is the principal. A gifted principal can work around difficult policies, find ways to stretch limited resources, raise expectations for every student, motivate current teachers and attract talented new ones, create an environment of respect, and energize an entire community.

While some homogeneous middle-class schools can almost run themselves, the principal's leadership in a diverse school is the major determining factor in whether the school functions as it should. Principals in diverse schools must use a more attentive and aggressive style of leadership than was required by the typical school of a decade or two ago. Without strong leadership paying attention to the varying needs of its students, the school will inevitably fail its students, parents, and community. However, when the principal takes on the role of leader to the fullest, a diverse school enriches all associated with it.

Once again, there is a need to bring in leadership that is more representative the populations being taught. Some 83 percent of principals are white. Even though the vast majority of educators are female, and far more mothers than fathers are active in schools nationwide, nearly 60 percent of principals are male.[2]

Principals at strong diverse schools take a fresh approach to leading their schools. They cannot rely on outdated management models. They lead by example, taking courageous actions and encouraging their staffs to follow. The principal sets the tone for the entire school, in ways that are very visible and in ways that may never be noticed.

Principals can be true leaders in numerous ways:

Set high academic standards for every student and develop targeted programs that help all students reach their potential.

A principal's most important role is serving as the instructional leader of the building. Whether carrying out one of their myriad duties—from hiring and supervising teachers to maintaining the building and assuring resources are sufficient—all the principal's actions must be geared toward one goal: strengthening students' skills and knowledge.

In a diverse school, that means focusing on the achievement of every student in the school. It begins with a belief that every child can succeed. It's too easy to blame lower student performance on changing demographics. Principals need to know who their students are, at what level they are achieving, and what it will take to propel them forward. "We cannot turn our heads away from anyone," says Juli Kwikkel, principal of East and West Elementary Schools in Storm Lake, Iowa. As a wave of new immigrants brought new faces to her schools, Kwikkel made a number of research-based changes to curriculum, scheduling and staffing, including adding programs geared to struggling readers, a daily ninety-minute reading block, and cross-grade reading groups. Kwikkel was recognized as a Distinguished Principal by the National Association of Elementary School Principals for her efforts.

Bowling Green Junior High in Kentucky has an array of initiatives to meet the needs of its students. Principal Joe Light states that the faculty is committed to ensuring that racial and ethnic minority students are moved into accelerated classes. The school also mainstreams special education students in regular classes. For at-risk students not quite ready for the leap to junior high, Bowling Green instituted a "Jump Start" program, bringing them in a week before other students. "When school starts, those kids feel like leaders because they know their way around, instead of feeling like they are lost," states Green. The school also fosters dreams of education beyond the school, working with Western Kentucky University to give students and their parents some campus experiences.

Be a proactive leader; set a tone for the building that is founded on respect of others.

Principals can have powerful influence on the way that students of different races and ethnicities get along in the school. Weak principals close their eyes to potential problems and assume that minor disagreements will just "work themselves out." They don't. They fester and become major problems, days, months, or years later.

A strong principal creates a school community where students know that each one is respected and that any disrespect, no matter how minor, will not be tolerated. This encourages students to listen to others' perspectives, and equally important, it makes them feel safe in sharing their own ideas and perspectives. To set a strong tone, the principal must be sensitive not only to what is obvious, but disrespect that may be subtler. In a school with students from all over the world, it may appear impossible to be sensitive to the needs of every student. As Annandale High Principal Donald Clausen explains, "You can't be aware of every cultural difference. But you can develop the sensitivity to ask the question, 'Is this a problem for you?'"

The Center for Research on Education, Diversity & Excellence at the University of California-Santa Cruz studied the effects of proactive school leaders on racial and ethnic harmony in schools across the country. They found that school leaders clearly "have the power to influence race relations in a positive direction." This strong leadership has many far-reaching implications. By promoting equity among students, school leadership improves relations among students and also increases academic achievement, improves student behavior, increases staff collaboration, and increases involvement of diverse parents, according to the study. In many successful diverse schools, the principals share their leadership in this regard with others who are committed to creating an environment of respectful learning, the report states, including faculty from other races or ethnicities.[3]

Side by Side School, a K–8 charter school in Norwalk, Connecticut, integrates respect for different cultures into the fabric of the school. Director Anne Alpert founded the school on the principle that a diverse environment benefits children and that every child can succeed "if the playing field is leveled," she says. The school population has a wide range of races, ethnicities, and economic backgrounds—from inner-city students living in the poorest neighborhoods to those from wealthy suburbs. "We try to shy away from boxed and packaged diversity programs, and instead weave the diversity throughout the curriculum," says Alpert.

In one project at Side by Side, third graders studied *Bread . . . from the Farm to the Bakery*. Taking advantage of the resources in their own community, the students visited local bakeries from many parts of the world, including Central America and Scandinavia. The students not only studied the different cultures represented by the bakeries, but also learned a respect for work involved in baking for the community. Family members were invited into the classroom to bring in baked goods typical of certain celebrations, to share the food, and discuss its role in their culture.

Identify the myths that color thinking in your own community and develop ways to address them publicly.

The principal, more than any other educational leader, has her finger on the pulse of the community. The principal should know what parents care about, what their concerns are, and what they think about the school. That goes as well for the residents who don't have school-age children, since they have a big say in school budgets as voters.

When I've done workshops for principals, some have asked how they are supposed to know what the community is thinking. The answer is by listening, even if you don't like what you hear. It's the only way to know what myths are poisoning your own community. Lots of principals see their role as informing the community. They forget the other side of the communications equation.

Principals need to talk to parents at every turn. They need to be visible members of parent organizations. They need to create informal ways to hear from parents, such as regular coffees in the principal's office or, even better, in neighborhood homes or meeting rooms. They need to respond to letters, e-mail, and phone calls. The parents reached through these avenues will not only relay what is on their minds, they will share what they are hearing from others in their neighborhoods and from parents at other schools.

Principals also need to be visible within the community. It's important to speak to the active local groups such as Rotary, Kiwanis, University

Women, NAACP, and key civic associations. Members of these groups will not only provide insight into the community's thinking, but they will often become major supporters of the school when they are brought in as partners. Superintendent Libia Gil of California's Chula Vista District believes it is critical for administrators to be visible in the community. She is on several boards herself, including serving as president of the YMCA, and she expects the principals in her district to be actively involved in community agencies. "Educational leadership is not only about learning within the four walls of the building. It is also about being a community leader," she says.

It's important to honestly analyze the neighborhood buzz. Are people concerned most that academics might not be rigorous at the school? Do they fear gang activity at the school? Are they worried that their children will not get enough attention because of the extra time given to language-minority children?

The most important thing first and foremost is that there are solid factual responses to the concerns. In a well-run diverse school, there are strong academic programs in place, challenging all the students in the school. So if academics are the concern, there are facts that the principal can use to address those concerns. Very often it's simply a matter of getting those facts into the hands of the concerned individuals. However, if the academic program at the school is basically weak, and administrators and faculty blame their problems on changing demographics instead of developing solutions, then the concerns of the community are no longer a myth, but a reality. The *first* step is to fix the problem. The second is to communicate the positive facts.

Annandale High School began a major outreach campaign in the mid-'90s to bring accurate information to a community reeling from negative press images and fears based on changing faces in the neighborhood. Our strategic plan included information meetings at all twelve of our feeder schools, increased opportunities for the high school students to interact with students in the lower grades, and outreach to community organizations such as Rotary and the Chamber of Commerce, as well as real estate agents.

A key part of our strategy was regular discussions among the team carrying this out to identify the most significant issues in the community at that time. We wanted to be proactive and address community concerns without participants having to push us. When we held our first few meetings, the most important issue was school safety. There had been a widely reported neighborhood fight that broke out along racial lines on a Sunday night and carried into the school on Monday morning. Even a year later, with many successful initiatives in place at the school, the community was solidly focused on ramifications of that incident. Ray Watson, Annandale High principal at the time, opened the outreach meetings by describing some of the positive programs in place at the school, such as our peer mediation program and the Heritage Day celebration. But he wasn't dismissing the fears of the community. He also delivered a nearly minute-by-minute account of what went on that Sunday night and Monday morning of the fight. When he was finished, everyone in the room realized that much of what they heard was wrong—for example, there was no gun in school as rumors held—and that the situation was not nearly as serious as they thought it was. Because Watson was so forthcoming, parents felt he was not hiding anything. The myth that the school was unsafe was successfully debunked in each of these meetings. We urged parents to ask us the tough questions in the room, so we could publicly dispel their concerns rather than leave them to their own whispered conversations. We also provided extensive information on the academic programs and vast extracurricular opportunities.

As we continued with our meetings over the next two years, the tone of the community changed. We could see that safety was no longer the number one issue. People now wanted to focus more on academics. So we changed the key messages and spent more time on the many academic strengths of the school. We brought Annandale students who had been accepted to Ivy League universities as speakers. I knew we had turned a corner when not one question from the audience dealt with safety.

Principals are in the primary position to be the trusted liaison between school and community. When they know their own neighborhood, they can address issues of concern honestly and directly. Truth is the best way to debunk a myth.

Seek out staff with open minds and a commitment to reaching every child.

When I asked Donald Clausen of Annandale High what was the most important role of a principal in a diverse school, he quickly replied, "hiring." "The hiring of staff that has a sensitivity to our population and has a desire to work in a diverse school is essential," Clausen says. He aggressively looks for teachers and administrators of racial and ethnic minorities. He also seeks out teachers who have lived extensively in another country or who speak another language. "This shows a sensitivity to other cultures," he says.

Don Montoya, principal at James Logan High School in Union City, California, believes that the teachers at his diverse school of 4,200 students must be open to the tough questions raised by diversity. "We have been trying as a school to talk about diversity more, and talk about what we need to do to make a difference for all our kids," Montoya says. He encourages his teachers to have "courageous conversations," in which they give short honest perspectives on a situation. "In 'courageous conversations,' you are saying you won't let things go anymore; you won't look the other way anymore," says Montoya. He believes the school needs teachers who are comfortable confronting the issues or at least willing to feel uncomfortable at times. "We're going to keep pushing forward. This is the way it's going to be."

At Dallas' Walnut Hill Elementary School, Principal Jo Anne Hughes always involves teachers in the interview process for their colleagues. The teachers appreciate the fact that Hughes considers their views. Equally important, they value the school culture of collaboration among the faculty and belief in the potential of each child, and they welcome the opportunity to communicate this philosophy to a potential hire. Hughes says hiring as a team further strengthens the collaborative spirit. "I've found that when I hire a teacher by myself, if she is not successful, the others will simply say I made a poor choice. However, when we select a new teacher as a team, everyone works harder to make sure the new teacher succeeds," says Hughes.

Provide opportunities for students to share their cultures in class and through schoolwide activities, including music, plays, and other presentations.

Students at diverse schools are one of its greatest resources. Students relish opportunities to share their own cultures and hear about those of other students. An effective principal finds many ways for students to share their heritage, both through class discussions and schoolwide events. Students at Annandale High are encouraged to share their life experiences, whether it is through English papers on their family history or art projects on their personal heroes. This sharing makes for a rich educational environment and also strengthens self-esteem.

In a well-run diverse school, there is a balance between seeing the similarities among students and cherishing the unique differences. Annandale High holds an annual festival each year, celebrating the diverse cultures of its student body. "On Heritage Day we acknowledged everyone's ethnicity and that enabled us to understand more about where they were coming from and gain greater respect for them," says graduate Melanie Pethcry. "It made it easier to work with everyone in class and open up to their perspectives." In recent years, Heritage Day has evolved into different formats to meet the needs of the school at that time. This year it is an evening program for the entire community.

Boise-Eliot Elementary School in Portland, Oregon, has sponsored a multicultural fair for the community for more than twenty years. Each classroom creates an exhibit for the curriculum-based fair, says teacher Katharine Johnson. In previous years the fair has focused on specific countries chosen by each classroom for year-long study. In recent years, the fair focused on celebrating the diversity of the school community itself. Students are encouraged to share family stories and recipes. The teachers at Boise-Eliot are leading the students in in-depth study, analyzing the makeup of the community, looking at business development trends, and recognizing local justice fighters. Funds raised by the fair go back into resources for future fairs and for purchasing supplies, such as books for the library by contemporary authors from different backgrounds.

Beverly Hills High School champions its diversity throughout a variety of school activities. "In this school, there is a value to having a different culture or different language," Principal Ben Bushman says. Not only does the school publish a traditional sixty-page literary magazine in English, it also publishes a foreign language literary magazine. The magazine, which has received national attention, includes articles in any language the student chooses.

Make sure every student has a strong connection with a caring adult—a parent, a teacher, a coach, or a mentor.

One of the most critical factors in facilitating student success is a connection with a caring adult. Many students are fortunate enough to have a parent or relative guiding their path through school. Others come from homes where parents don't provide that critical connection because they have struggles of their own, or too many overwhelming responsibilities from work or family, or they simply don't know how to help their children succeed in a school system that is foreign to them.

It's easy for adults to make connections with the school "stars." However, it's often the students at the other end of the spectrum, the ones who are either so quiet they are ignored or so troublesome they are avoided, who desperately need that link. Logan High School's Montoya is committed to reaching every student. He is most concerned about those students who are at the lowest level of achievement. "We have to ask, 'Why is that kid not connecting with school? What can we do differently to make a connection between that kid and an adult to make a difference academically?'" Montoya says.

Montoya instructed every teacher at Logan to make a connection with five students from the lowest twentieth percentile in their eighth-period class. The teacher's task is to build a relationship with each one, including making contact with the parents. The teachers discuss their successes and struggles in cross-curricular meetings. There have been some immediate successes, including an improvement in attendance. Montoya supports the teachers in their efforts with professional development opportunities, including workshops led by minority faculty members, since many of the students are members of racial and ethnic minorities. "Can you imagine the results schoolwide if five of our lowest-achieving students in every class turn around their performance?" says Montoya.

Create opportunities that increase interactions among students of different races and ethnic groups.

It's no secret that barriers between students of different races and ethnic backgrounds are broken down most quickly in extracurricular activities. Members of the basketball team practicing for the tournament, actors rehearsing for a play, fledgling journalists pushing to beat the deadline for the school paper, all get to know each other as individuals working toward a common goal. The principal should be an avid supporter of a wide variety of extracurricular activities—not just the glamorous ones like football—and encourage all students to participate. This role is even more important with students from ethnic minorities. Many immigrant parents feel that these after-school activities are just distractions from study, while research clearly shows that involvement in extracurricular activities strengthens student academic performance,[4] and reduces opportunities for students to experiment with unhealthy behaviors.[5] Their students miss out on both academic and social levels by not participating.

"These activities do more than generate school spirit," says Pedro Noguera of the Harvard Graduate School of Education. "They give kids a chance to get to know each other and break down some of the distance." The key is to "expand who can be involved," says Noguera. While some schools have an array of activities for students to choose from, others have only limited opportunities. There are schools where only a small numbers of gifted athletes can play sports, Noguera says as an example. He urges principals to provide other avenues, such as intramurals, along with clubs serving wide-ranging interests.

Develop outreach programs that break down barriers to parent participation.

It is important to know your own community. What works in one neighborhood will not work in another. Fairfax County School Board member Cathy Belter remembers traveling to south Florida to work with parents on math education when she was a vice president of the National PTA in the late '80s. To Belter's surprise, the school principal set the parent meeting for the middle of the day. Belter knew that a midday meeting in her home community in northern Virginia would not be well attended. But this principal knew that the parents in her community, which was largely Hispanic, felt evenings were family time and they would not come to a meeting at night. The principal added another incentive to the daytime meeting, making it a potluck luncheon where the parents were encouraged to bring their favorite dish for a fun competition judged by one of the food editors from the *Miami Herald*. Attendance overflowed.

Susan Akroyd, whose diverse elementary school in Fairfax County sponsors a Family Center in the community, says, "When it is difficult, for many reasons, to get parents into the school, it is important to search for ways in which to bring 'the school' to the parents and family members." The center provides parents with a range of classes for themselves and their children right in the heart of the neighborhood. Akroyd and other school officials are regular visitors at the center.

Principal Jo Anne Hughes wanted to find new ways to work with African American parents in her Dallas elementary school. She held a meeting with these parents to express her concern about the gap between test scores from the African American and white students in the school and asked the parents for their help. Hughes said that the face-to-face meeting raised the level of awareness among the parents, and many became more involved with the school. Some parents came up with new ways to help. "One parent said she doesn't have the time to come to school on a regular basis, but she was happy to mentor a student over the phone," Hughes said. The school arranged for that mentoring relationship. Test scores have begun rising among the African American students, shrinking the achievement gap.

Give parents substantive opportunities to be involved in the school.

While some parents face cultural or language barriers making it difficult to connect with schools, other parents are simply victims of hectic lives in which they are attempting to balance many family and work commitments. To take the important step of becoming active in the school, they must feel that their involvement is not only welcomed, but valued. One way to gain more parent participation is to bring parents in as collaborators. This means the principal truly has to share some of the power, but there is a lot to be gained from a strong partnership.

I always credit former Annandale Principal Ray Watson with starting me on my many hours of public involvement at Annandale High. In the fall of 1992, I went to a Back-to-School Night for my daughter. There was a lot of negative chatter about the school in the neighborhood, but all I saw was a great school. PTA President Mary Gormley had given a rousing speech that night, recounting all the strengths of Annandale and asking each of us to be "public relations agents" in our own neighborhoods. I decided this was my moment to get involved in the school. I went up to Gormley at 10:00 P.M. and said, "I'm a communications consultant. I'd be willing to help in any way I can." By the time I got home, there was a phone call for me. Gormley and Watson invited me to a meeting in the principal's office at 9:00 the next morning. At the meeting, Watson told me how much he appreciated my stepping forward. "Tell us what we can do to work together," he said. From that moment on, I had the complete support of both Watson and his successor Donald Clausen. They both welcomed me in as a partner. In return, I was careful to remember that I was a parent leader, not the educational leader of the school, and that my first responsibility was to support the principal's efforts. This doesn't mean I haven't been honest or forthright in advocating my positions with the school leadership, but the relationship has been one of mutual trust and respect.

When parents are valued, they are willing to make extraordinary contributions. Merrill and Mark Shugoll, parents of an Annandale High student, donated the services of their marketing research firm to help assess student attitudes toward learning and the school. They conducted a series of focus group interviews with students and a comprehensive schoolwide student survey. The cost of this would have been staggering. The results of the services donated by Shugoll Research have been invaluable in planning programs to meet our students needs. "When someone suggested this idea, I was thrilled to be able to do it, " Merrill said. "I really respect those who take on the traditional volunteer leadership roles, but I'm not always comfortable in those roles. I felt competent donating my professional services."

Perform miracles, large and small, on a daily basis.

In a well-run diverse school, the principal is often viewed as a miracle worker. "When she needs something done and can't hire someone, she finds a volunteer. When she needs to buy something and doesn't have the budget for it, she finds a business that will donate it," says parent Mollie Fox in describing Gladys Vaccarezza, principal of Chicago's Blaine Elementary School. "She knows every student's name, their room number, their grade level, and their parents," adds assistant principal Geraldine Kearns.

The best principals do work miracles every day. They find solutions when others would find the problem hopeless. Their ideas are creative, but practical. At Blaine Elementary, Vaccarezza displays that can-do attitude in countless ways every day. Believing in the value of small class size, Vaccarezza hires additional teachers with any discretionary funds she is provided by the state. She fills in what's needed with grants, donations, and volunteers. When teachers have innovative ideas, Vaccarezza works hard to turn them into reality. With grants from a variety of sources, including the Chicago Foundation for Education and Learning Power Grants from the Chicago Public Schools, librarian Patricia Dempsey led the effort to transform the school's outmoded library into a library media center. The cheerful rooms include a separate primary center that not only serves the younger school students but also neighborhood families with two- and three-year olds who visit for story hour. Vaccarezza's support was instrumental. Turning down a job offer to become a region librarian for one of the six ninety-five-school regions in Chicago, Dempsey says enthusiastically Blaine Elementary is where she wants to be.

Vaccarezza has also implemented innovative schoolwide initiatives. Many in the Blaine community are Spanish speakers learning English as a new language. Instead of focusing on the needs of only the Hispanic students, Vaccarezza chose to teach the entire community Spanish. Each class, from preschool through third grade (with plans to build this program through the eighth grade) has a block of Spanish instruction each day. Where did Vaccarezza find teachers for this program? She connected with the Spanish Embassy, which sponsors the program. The embassy sends two visiting teachers to work with the students. As enthusiastic about the program as the Blaine community, the embassy has been working with two well-respected high schools nearby to continue the program from Blaine. Parents aren't left out of the program; two volunteers provide classes for parents—one teaching Spanish and one teaching English to Spanish speakers. Vaccarezza, who learned English as an adult herself when she emigrated from Argentina, spurs the parents on. With this and other initiatives, Vaccarezza has stemmed the flow to private schools from the middle-class homes in her neighborhood.

The principal is the rock-bottom foundation of the school. Attacking the tasks at hand with vigor and optimism, a principal can bring a diverse school to life and motivate all around her to do their part to help. At the end of the day, she'll sleep well, and she'll deserve it.

NOTES

1. Richard Riley, "The 21st Century Principal: Opportunities and Challenges. An Interview with U.S. Secretary of Education Richard W. Riley and NAESP Executive Director Vincent L. Ferrardino," *Principal Magazine* 80, no. 1 (September 2000): 6–12.

2. *Public and Private School Principals in the United States: A Statistical Profile, 1993–94* (NCES 97-455), National Center for Educational Statistics, U.S. Department of Education.

3. Rosemary C. Henze, *Leading for Diversity: How School Leaders Achieve Racial and Ethnic Harmony* (Santa Cruz: Center for Research on Education, Diversity & Excellence, University of California at Santa Cruz, June 2000).

4. *Extracurricular Participation and Student Engagement*, National Center for Education Statistics, U.S. Department of Education, June 1995.

5. See "The National Cross-Site Evaluation of High-Risk Youth Programs," Center for Substance Abuse Prevention, Substance Abuse and Mental Health Services Administration, DHHS Publication No. SMA-25-01, January 2002.

TEACHERS: REACHING FOR EVERY CHILD

A blind political science professor (at Brooklyn College), Louis War-soff, became interested in me and we had long talks. . . . From Professor Warsoff I learned that white people were not really different from me. I loved formal debating particularly, and once after I starred in a match, he told me "You ought to go into politics." I was astonished at his naiveté. "Proffy," I said, "you forget two things. I'm black—and I'm a woman."

—Shirley Chisholm, former member of Congress, *A Special Relationship: Our Teachers and How We Learned*[1]

Education truly comes down to one magical connection—that link between teacher and child. A gifted teacher can reach students against all odds. A teacher without that spark can lose an entire class, even with a room overflowing with books, displays, and the latest technology.

It's not easy to be a teacher. The first few years are particularly demanding. Some teachers have a few successful years, and believe they have mastered the profession. They resist change—new strategies, new techniques seem unnecessary and burdensome. But teachers, like their students, need to be lifelong learners. Research is always identifying new ways to reach children, such as the latest research on how the brain functions.

The problem of teachers who refuse to grow as professionals becomes a real crisis in a diverse school. The old ways of pedagogy just aren't good enough to reach a community of diverse learners. Change isn't easy, but it is the only option if teachers are going to live up to the ideals of their profession.

My husband, Larry, has been an educator with Fairfax County Public Schools for three decades, as a teacher, a trainer, and an administrator. One of the tasks he enjoys most is working with faculties on helping them differentiate their instruction to meet the varying needs of students. "The faster the faculty can get past blaming students for their problems and recognize that they have to teach differently, the more successful the school is," he says. "Teachers cannot present information in just one way today; they have to introduce concepts in a variety of ways." Larry helped organize Fairfax County's Reach to Teach conference that offered the county's elementary teachers techniques for identifying what students know and guidance on how to use a range of teaching methods to meet the students' needs.

"We need teachers who are open to the challenges and benefits of diversity," Larry says. "When teachers are excited about teaching in diverse classrooms, they push themselves to find ways to reach all the students in their classrooms. Differentiating instruction isn't easy, but there is nothing as rewarding as seeing all your students engaged in learning."

Teachers need to create a community of learners within their classroom. In this environment, every student feels significant as an individual with something important to contribute. Students truly feel valued if they are encouraged to share themselves—their backgrounds, their experiences, their store of knowledge—in the classroom. In a diverse classroom, this is a resource beyond any other.

Today's educational system would benefit from teachers of diverse backgrounds but there is a shortage of teachers from minority groups, exacerbated by the shortage of all teachers. Every principal I spoke with was disappointed that he or she could not find more teachers of color. Most principals realize that minority teachers are important not only for students from diverse backgrounds, but for all students. Teachers from racial and ethnic minorities bring new insights and experiences to the classroom, break down stereotypes, and serve as important role models.

All teachers can work to bring out the best in every child. There are a number of critical strategies toward that goal:

Examine your own attitudes toward people who are different from you.

Yvonne Freeman directs the graduate teaching program in bilingual education at Fresno Pacific University, working closely with her husband, David, who directs the Teachers of English to Speakers of Other Languages (TESOL) program. They find that one of the biggest obstacles to teaching effectively in a diverse school is that most teachers haven't fully explored their own attitudes toward students and families who have different backgrounds than their own.

Yvonne asks her graduate students to conduct an extensive case study of one of their own students. "Teachers are sometimes amazed that they didn't realize how well their kids do certain things. In the beginning, they often don't know if the child can read and write in their first language. Awareness helps overcome a negative attitude that is often a subconscious one," she says.

Some teachers unwittingly place greater value on students who have parents who "act right"—basically as the teacher hopes or expects. This asset is labeled "social capital" in the research community. White middle-class families know what schools expect of them and are willing to fulfill the role, because they come from backgrounds that provided them with relevant skills and experiences. They generally come to the school with a more trusting attitude, their personal experiences not tarnished by the racism or prejudice faced by minority parents.[2]

This extra asset of the white middle-class families doesn't have to translate into preferential treatment in the school, however. Educators have a choice in how they value the capital and how it influences their decision making in class. Tough questions need to be asked. Do white middle-class students get into gifted programs because their parents know how to fill out the forms correctly and advocate appropriately for their children? Are students of color and those from lower-income backgrounds placed in low reading groups because their parents aren't as deferential to teachers? To truly create a classroom where equity reigns, teachers must be willing to take a serious look at their reactions to students and their families who have different experiences than their own.

Have high expectations for every student.

This is where it all starts in a diverse school. The teacher who succeeds in a diverse classroom is the one who enters with a belief that every student can achieve. Alan Weintraut teaches journalism and film studies at Annandale High, and he is the advisor to the student newspaper. When he came to the school, the student newspaper was a mediocre publication barely read by the students. Within three years, the *A-Blast* was ranked among the top ten in the nation.[3] In his seven years at the school, four of Weintraut's students were named Virginia High School Journalist of the Year.

"If you spend time one on one with each learner and find out what is going to motivate them, everyone will be able to reach a rising bar," says Weintraut. He works hard at finding the key that sparks the interest of each of his students. He often spends Sunday evening watching movies that he feels may strike a particular chord with one of his film studies students. Under his leadership, the school began hosting a schoolwide film festival where his students present their own work. A number of his students have been so engaged by his class that they have further studied film production in college. "All students have an innate desire to succeed, but they also want someone to take an interest in what they find interesting. Regardless of creed, culture, background, birth nation, or gender, the kids who *want* to do well, will."

Susan Collins, whose daughter spent four years in Weintraut's journalism classes, says,

> It's a parent's dream that the teacher would recognize that each child has gifts and talents and that they can stretch themselves to meet higher goals. He erases all the lines of sex and race and creed and just sees the pure person in his class. He believes every child can grow and learn, and they do. You can see how much the student newspaper improves from September to May each year, as the kids in his classes develop. They finish school as seniors believing that they can tackle the next step, whatever it is.

Encourage students and families to share their personal experiences in class, through discussions, artwork, and essays.

A healthy classroom is founded on the principle of equity of opportunity. By creating an environment where every child can participate as a valued member of the class, the teacher enriches education on many levels. "Nothing is more interesting to kids than each other," says teacher Kate Andreatta, who now works with the National Education Association. In her elementary classroom, she used every opportunity to share all the knowledge, experiences, and customs of her students and their families throughout the curriculum. Andreatta team-taught an innovative multiage class that combined first, second, and third grades at Woodrow Wilson Elementary School in Binghamton, New York. "It was an amazing experience," she says.

Effective teachers in diverse schools will enthusiastically tell you how the richness of student contributions inspires their own teaching. Katharine Johnson of Boise-Eliot Elementary School in Portland, Oregon, not only encourages students to share their personal experiences, she also invites family members into her second grade class when she does her unit on immigration patterns. To make sure every family can participate, even those who don't have details about their own immigration history, she loosely defines immigration as a change in geography. "It's clear to me that student learning is more alive," Johnson says, "which could be because I am more excited about teaching this way."

By encouraging students to express themselves through ways that validate their own life experiences, teachers can tap into student talents that might have remained locked away. Shukri Sindi was a reserved student in art teacher Joyce Weinstein's class at Annandale High, putting in a halfhearted effort. Weinstein began talking with him about his background. She learned he had spent three years in a Kurdish refugee camp in Turkey. Hoping to bring out the unexpressed talent she saw, Weinstein encouraged him to use his own life experiences in his art. Sindi began transferring his searing memories to the canvas, with remarkable results. He not only won several major art competitions, he earned a scholarship to Pratt Institute's architecture program. At the same time, his work opened other students' eyes to experiences far beyond their own.

Creative teachers look beyond the boundaries of their own classroom for resources. "A journalism teacher has a big advantage in a diverse school. When I tell students every student has a story to tell, it's really true here," says Annandale's Weintraut. In Advanced Placement Journalism, each student must write a profile of an eleventh-grade classmate that Weintraut has chosen at random. With a school population of students from more than eighty nationalities, the matchups prove interesting. "Even though my students are around diversity every day, they haven't had the opportunity before to delve into the lives of someone so different," he says. "This is a great journalistic challenge for them. They have to observe the person on three occasions, establish rapport, use fine-tuned interview skills, find an interesting angle, and write a descriptive piece." The students chosen are almost always willing subjects, eager to tell their stories. Profiles illuminate many personal challenges, from stories of families who escaped native countries huddling on a boat, to students who date outside their cultures despite their parents' strong disapproval. The profiles themselves are published in the school newspaper, further building community among students as they get to know each other beyond the surface exchange of greetings.

Use stories and examples that include people from a variety of backgrounds and cultures.

Diversity of experience should be reflected in classroom materials at all times, not just when students discuss their own backgrounds. For too many years, textbooks and curriculum material reflected only one culture and one set of experiences. This left many feeling alienated from the educational system. To build on the strengths of the diversity in today's classrooms, teachers need to make sure that their lessons are broadly representative of different experiences, including achievements of people from different cultures and illustrations that represent people of color. "Teaching from a range of perspectives will prepare students from diverse groups to work together in a truly unified nation," according to educator and author James Banks.[4]

It's not always easy to find the resources that broaden the scope of classroom teaching. Some teachers who have been gathering classroom materials for years may have to expand collections they considered to be "complete." But publishers are making available an increasing number of textbooks and supplementary literature reflective of different cultures. These in turn can inspire discussions that include many universal experiences. There are also new resources appearing daily on the Internet, including a comprehensive website with links to additional resources from the U.S. Department of Education.[5] Teachers need to advocate for additional classroom and library materials to support this goal.

It largely boils down to an attitude about how materials should be presented and discussed. Sometimes it's as simple as buying construction paper in varying shades of beige and brown to use for children's faces on a bulletin board. Sometimes it's digging for the stories on lesser known heroes, like Benjamin Banneker, the son of a slave credited with recreating the detailed plans for the new city of Washington after his hot-headed boss, architect Pierre L'Enfant, was dismissed from the project and took the plans with him.

A teacher can open up horizons and inspire students' in-depth thinking through the choice of literature and facilitated classroom discussion. A story like *Knots on a Counting Rope*, the tale of a Native American grandfather who uses a counting rope to help his blind grandson understand the passage of time, can ignite a discussion of cultures, physical challenges, and the relationship between young and old.[6] Or a teacher can begin a dialogue on family visits in different cultures after reading *The Relatives Came*, a humorous tale of relatives from a rural farm visiting their suburban relations.[7] For older students, it may be a discussion of the Nazi's attempt at "ethnic cleansing" and similar experiences in other cultures, inspired by reading Elie Wiesel's piercing story of the Holocaust, "Night."[8]

Create a classroom environment where students feel comfortable expressing their ideas.

Every other student from a strong diverse school whom I interviewed emphasized that students were encouraged to speak their minds, listen to others, and think critically in the classroom. Teachers in these schools, supported by their principals, created an environment in which students felt comfortable presenting their own perspectives, no matter how challenging their ideas might be. That way everyone got to lay their ideas on the table, hear responses, and integrate the other perspectives into their own thinking.

Taylor Butler who attends Murrah High School in Jackson, Mississippi, put it this way: "We don't just sit in class learning to memorize dates or how to do equations. We learn how to analyze, challenge, and adapt this knowledge to life. No one forces us to conform." In Jackson, many of the middle-class white students attend private academies set up to avoid integration of the public schools. Butler is grateful for the opportunity to be in an academic environment that encourages divergent thought. "My friends from the private schools all come from the same religious background, go to the same youth group, have the same parental style. But they will soon be in society where they will find the opposite extreme. Their schools give them no room for change," she says.

Teachers have extraordinary power within their classroom walls. A classroom where every child feels valued not only contributes to individual academic growth, but researchers find that it also connects kids to the school itself, which is a powerful protective factor against a number of risky behaviors. An analysis of data from the National Longitudinal Study of Adolescent Health, which surveyed 90,000 students in grades 7–12 in 80 U.S. communities, revealed that students with a strong connection to school were less likely to drink, take illegal drugs, commit violent acts, experience emotional distress, or become pregnant.[9] The leading factor in developing this connection to school? The way the teacher runs the classroom. Strong connections develop when the teacher consistently acknowledges all students and gives students the chance to participate in management of the class, such as having input on classroom rules and doing regular jobs to support the teacher. These classrooms are most likely to exist in schools where administrators set clear expectations for individual responsibility and conflict resolution among students, the researchers found.[10]

Make sure you know something about every child in the class.
It's easy to know the top achievers in the class and it's necessary to know the most disruptive students. But sitting somewhere else in the classroom are the students who are quiet, get by, and don't cause trouble. They are often the ones who are internally screaming to be noticed.

One of the groups often overlooked by teachers are students from ethnic communities that have good English schools, says Gil Garcia of the U.S. Department of Education's National Institute on the Education of At-Risk Students. "Just because these students come to school with good English, doesn't mean they are not in need of attention. Many of them live in multicultural and multilingual communities. Teachers need to understand what makes them tick, what makes them respond to teaching. They do bring cultural resources to the school that need to be recognized," Garcia says.

It's trite, but true. Teachers do hold the future in their hands. We don't know who will be a Supreme Court justice, who will discover a miracle drug, who will write a Pulitzer Prize-winning book, who will teach in a challenging school, and who will be a community leader. All children deserve the chance to become all they can be. And that takes a teacher who believes in the capability of every student, who confirms they are all valued participants in the classroom, and who encourages their independent thought.

NOTES

1. Shirley Chisholm, *A Special Relationship: Our Teachers and How We Learn*, ed. John C. Board (Wainscott, N.Y.: Pushcart Press, 1991), 298.

2. Annette Lareau and Erin McNamara Horvat, "Moments of Social Inclusion and Exclusion: Race, Class and Cultural Capital in Family-Social Relationships," *Sociology of Education* 72 (January 1999): 37–53.

3. National Scholastic Press Association (Conventions Best of Show).

4. James A. Banks, "Educating for Diversity," *Educational Leadership* 51, no. 8 (May 1994).

5. www.ed.gov [accessed 15 June 2002].

6. Bill Martin Jr., *Knots on a Counting Rope* (New York: Holt, 1987).

7. Cynthia Rylant, *The Relatives Came* (New York: Bradbury Press, 1985).

8. Elie Wiesel, *Night* (New York: Bantam, 1982).

9. R. W. Blum and P. Mann Rinehart, *Reducing the Risk: Connections That Make a Difference in the Lives of Youth* (Minneapolis: Division of General Pediatrics and Adolescent Health, University of Minnesota, 1998).

10. R. W. Blum and C. A. McNeely, *Improving the Odds: The Untapped Power of Schools to Improve the Health of Teens* (Minneapolis: Center for Adolescent Health and Development, University of Minnesota, 2000).

PARENTS: THE CRITICAL CONNECTION

Community empowerment is everybody getting involved for a common cause. It is a fallacy that all parents do not want to participate in their children's education. Generally, the situation is one of parents not knowing *how* to get involved.

—Ivy H. Lovelady, "The Day the Mill Closed"[1]

The PTA president of a very diverse elementary school bubbled over with enthusiasm as she talked to me about the exciting things happening to strengthen parent involvement in her school. She talked about the efforts to welcome parents who have recently arrived in this country. She talked about the free events for the entire community on weekends, including the international dinner that included a book fair, speakers, and artists. She talked about opportunities that the school created for parents who don't speak English to come in and help with projects once a week. She talked about the new community center that is staffed with parent liaisons for several nationality groups, including Indian, Spanish, and one for the American-born families.

PTA President Carolyn Tabarini sees her role as "raising the comfort level" for all parents at Groveton Elementary in Fairfax County, Virginia, no matter what the obstacles. I was struck by the types of programs she did *not* discuss. I said to Tabarini, "I didn't hear you talk about any programs designed specifically for kids like yours." "And you never will," she said.

It's not that Tabarini's children don't benefit from the school. She could not say enough about the growth of her children, one of whom is now in a diverse middle school. Groveton has a strong emphasis on academic challenge, particularly literacy. But the biggest plus for Tabarini is the opportunity for her children to interact with students from nearly thirty nations. "My kids rarely come home and say someone moved here from New York or St. Louis. Instead, they tell me someone just moved here from China or Bosnia or Botswana. There is never a comment that the other child doesn't speak English. The children always seem to be able to communicate." Commenting that some middle-class children have never been exposed to people from other races or from low-income homes, Tabarini notes, "My kids are comfortable sitting down next to anybody."

Tabarini's comments illustrate the distinct characteristic of parent organizations that truly build community in diverse schools. There is a commitment on the part of the parents who are actively involved to strengthen the entire school by increasing opportunities for all parents to become involved with their students' education. It is true that most of these parents initially became involved to support their own children. But in a well-run diverse school, the commitment to building community becomes so strong that active parents start thinking in broad terms of helping all parents, particularly those who don't have the experience and skills to negotiate the complex American school system. They recognize that by increasing opportunities for these parents to be involved, they not only help those families, but they build links among all families in the community, strengthening the school culture, and increasing opportunities for growth for themselves and their children.

The research on the importance of parent involvement in a child's education is striking. Students with involved families generally do better in school, stay in school longer, and continue their studies after high school.[2] For many parents, being involved in the school is a given—their parents went to parent-teacher conferences, attended school plays, chaperoned trips, cheered for sports teams, and so, of course, will they. For other parents, the connection has never been made. Maybe they didn't do well in school themselves so they don't feel comfortable talking with school officials. Maybe the school is just a foreign place, filled with people who act and think different than they do, perhaps even speaking a language they don't feel competent in.

I've heard many parent leaders in diverse schools talk about their own experience in solving a sticky school problem for their child. It often takes several conversations with the teacher, the guidance counselor, maybe even the principal. In the end when it is resolved, the parents sit back and imagine trying to do this if you are not comfortable advocating for your children with school officials. It is often a motivating force that drives parent leaders to strategize ways to break down obstacles so that every parent can be a partner in key decisions that affect their child in school as well as at home.

Thus, many parent organizations in well-run diverse schools see one of their primary roles as ensuring that all parents feel a part of the school. Programs are geared to meeting the needs of many different families, not just the ones who find it easy to take part in the traditional ways. Everyone, from every background, benefits from this approach.

Here are some ways that parents can support both the student and parent communities of the school:

Don't blame other parents for not participating; instead, seek out new ways to provide alternatives for parents who are not served by current parent outreach.

While many schools work hard to build community, some are stuck in the us-versus-them mentality. It is often seen in neighborhoods where the demographics are changing, and the existing community doesn't quite know how to respond appropriately. The parents hold the tried-and-true PTA events—a meeting on a Tuesday morning or Wednesday night, advertised through a newsletter that goes out in English. Since basically the white middle-class parents show up, they sit around and question the parenting commitment of the parents who don't come. The business meeting focuses on things that largely benefit the children of those who are there—after all, they are the ones who bothered to show up and prove they care. Leadership stays in the hands of parents who have only one set of experiences. Other parents feel uncomfortable trying to break into the established group of "insiders." And thus the cycle perpetuates itself—the meetings are increasingly run by and for the dominant white culture, with the parents from racial and ethnic minorities finding the meetings less accessible and relevant to their needs. Alienation among the groups sets in.

It is only when parent groups break out of the mold of seeing just the needs of their own children that community-building begins. Active parents in these schools seek new ways to bring more parents into the school community, learn from one another, help one another, and strengthen the school. Students in strong diverse schools already have the opportunity to interact across races and ethnic groups because it is part of their everyday school life. Parents, however, can easily isolate themselves into their own distinct groups. Yet parents can move beyond learned patterns and create opportunities for interaction so they can personally grow from meeting parents of diverse backgrounds and can strengthen the school community.

In an effort to break out of limiting patterns, the Annandale High PTA handed out parent surveys in five languages at Back-to-School Night and at special parent nights for students who were English-language learners. The surveys told us first and foremost that all parents share a common interest in and concerns about their teenagers. They also told us that many parents find it difficult to attend programs on weekday nights, so we began holding an International Dinner on Sunday evenings. What a heartwarming sight to see entire families in their native dress coming to the school with overflowing bowls of their traditional recipes, finally having an opportunity to be a part of school life! These dinners evolved into a "Bravo" dinner that featured graduates who had succeeded in overcoming many obstacles to reach their academic and career goals. In later years, we received a grant to host special parent programs for our major minority populations in community rooms in the heart of their neighborhoods, providing guidance on how to help their children in the school, translated into the relevant language.

The PTA at Annandale High also sponsors programs that help us all learn together. We've held panel discussions with representatives from several of the ethnic groups at our school presenting the special challenges that they face in maintaining their own culture while their families become a part of the new culture that surrounds them. Those of us in the audience had our eyes opened as we learned that a simple sleepover invitation—a staple of American childhood—can be a real crisis for a parent from a culture that traditionally allows children to visit only their close relatives. Yet it was clear that many concerns crossed cultures, from teenage dating to underage drinking.

The PTA at Rosemont Elementary School in Gaithersburg, Maryland, hosts free family fun nights for their diverse neighborhood. "We didn't want cost to be a hurdle, so the PTA pays for the programs," says PTA President Jane Rice. Pizza and soda are provided at cost. Flyers for these nights, as well as all PTA activities, are translated into Spanish, the predominant second language of the neighborhood. The recent magic show was a big hit in the community, attracting about 300. The school's Hispanic liaison noted that many of the Hispanic parents were talking enthusiastically about the show days later.

Respect differences, even if you are uncomfortable with them. Don't expect others to be like you.

The first step toward building a community in a diverse school is recognizing that the strength of the school is in the differences people bring to the environment. "As a life-long resident of this area, I and my family consider the cultural diversity a real gift," says Carolyn Tabarini of the neighborhood surrounding Groveton Elementary School. "There are not many places we can meet so many people from so many lands without getting on a plane!"

Andrea Sobel, whose daughter, Gina, attends Annandale High, says that they both believe "the importance of a school like Annandale High does not stem from a notion of 'color blindness.' We are not, and I do not believe that anyone is or should be, color blind. We believe Annandale works as a diverse school more because it is *not* color blind."

"Diversity is not to be ignored, accepted, or tolerated—this leads to schools with a tourism view of multiculturalism," Sobel says. "Diversity is to be sought out, identified, and celebrated. A multicultural school offers every student from every cultural, linguistic and ethnic background an opportunity to be themselves amidst a sea of others different from themselves. It allows individual students and families to express pride in who they are within a community of other proud individuals and families. It encourages dialogue and increased understanding of those very differences that make us all unique rather than trying to blend as one— we are not one! Rather we are a community of many—contributing to the growth of the community."

Accepting differences among people is not always easy. One of the striking features of the Annandale community is that it includes many families who fled violence in countries all over the world—from both sides of the conflicts. We have families from all sides of the ethnic disputes in the Balkans, who came to the United States at the height of "ethnic cleansing." We have students from both sides of internal political conflicts in Central America and Africa. We have students from every major Arab nation and the Palestinian territories, as well as Israelis, and American-born Jews and Arabs. The students manage to learn rapidly how to interact and respect each other. The adults need to follow their lead.

Find ways to bring the community together.

Parent and business leader Andy Shallal looks for every opportunity to build community. He has been president of the PTA in his daughters' elementary and middle schools and is an active supporter of the high school even though his older daughter is just now entering ninth grade. Believing in the importance of taking a broad view, Shallal also was a founding member of the Annandale Community Coalition, a youth advocacy organization for students K–12.

One of the most meaningful events for Shallal is the annual Kids Against Drugs and Alcohol (KADA) festival, sponsored by the Coalition. Held at Annandale High School, the Saturday event includes students of all ages for a day of games, motivational speeches, and workshops for students and parents. "KADA involves the whole community and emphasizes the connectivity of all schools," says Shallal. "It's a great celebration of the community: having vibrant, healthy kids come together with community members, health care workers, fire fighters, police officers, all with the goal of taking care of our kids."

Shallal also lends his resources and expertise as a local restaurateur to support the school community. He frequently donates catered meals for students and families for community events, such as a coalition-sponsored retreat for student leaders. "Providing the students with a quality luncheon is one way to show them how much we value their insights," says Shallal.

As Annandale High School was being renovated, Shallal saw another opportunity to strengthen the school community. Active in the National Restaurant Association, Shallal views "restaurants as the cornerstone of communities. They are not only an economic engine, they also are a place where people meet and gather," Shallal says. The high school already had a well-respected culinary arts program. With full support of Principal Donald Clausen, Shallal began working with the school's architect to create a restaurant in the school and build in restaurant-quality cooking equipment. The seventy-seat full-service restaurant, to be run by students, will provide real-life experience in food preparation and service, as well as management and accounting. Students will have the opportunity to gain accreditation in the hospitality field.

Volunteer to come into your child's school to talk about your own heritage and unique life experiences.

Many schools recognize the great resources that parents can provide to bring the curriculum to life. They welcome parents in to the classroom to share their family history and traditions, as well as personal experiences. It is important to take advantage of the opportunities, no matter what your personal experiences. To understand and respect differences, students need to learn that everyone has an important story to tell.

I have a friend whose father was killed in action during the Vietnam War. Her mother, of the generation that deferred to male business skills, didn't even know how to balance a checkbook. Suddenly she was faced with not only raising her children, but also supporting them and running the family home. Linda frequently speaks to high school classes, giving firsthand testimony to life with a military father in a small southern town during the Vietnam War era and the growing awareness of women's rights in her family.

Share in the family traditions of others and make your home a welcome environment for people of other races and ethnic backgrounds.

For my family, one of the greatest joys of being part of a diverse community is learning about fascinating cultures as invited guests in traditions, ceremonies, and celebrations. We've celebrated the birthday of Buddha at a Buddhist Temple; attended Palm Sunday services at a black Baptist Church; participated in an interfaith service that included Catholics, Protestants, Jews, and Hindus; dined on Middle Eastern cuisine at the home of Arab friends; decorated Christmas trees; shared Easter dinners; and had many, many wonderful discussions with friends of different faiths and heritages. We love sitting down and talking with students from different backgrounds whom we meet through our children. Recently my daughter attended a Sikh ceremony at the home of her friend Jaspreet as his family moved into their new home, celebrating along with dozens of relatives and friends including some who had come from Michigan and California, as well as India.

Similarly, we share our heritage whenever we can. Every year, we invite non-Jewish friends to join us for our Passover Seder, our family's most treasured holiday. We invite our children's friends over to eat latkes and play dreidle during Chanukah. We have built a *succah*—an outdoor booth celebrating the Jewish harvest festival of *Succot*—with fellow participants in a Jewish-Muslim dialogue. My son, an opera student, includes songs of his Jewish heritage in his community recitals.

We work to build bridges whenever we can. A few years ago, we arranged for our friend Andy Shallal, an Iraqi-American from a Muslim family, to speak at our synagogue. A fellow congregant came up to me and said she envied my friendship. She told me there is a Muslim mother she often sees in her neighborhood, but she doesn't know quite what to say to her. It made me sad that our neighborhoods are filled with people who could share so much, but don't have the skills to maneuver the uncharted waters of interacting with people of different backgrounds. Diverse schools provide students and parents valuable opportunities to bridge these differences, but you have to take advantage of them.

Mentor a student.

A mentor program can be a powerful tool, particularly in a diverse school. We all know the important role that one adult can play in the life of a child, yet some students simply don't have an adult who can assume the responsibility of guider and role model. "I have seen the positive impact that one individual can have on another," says parent Andrea Sobel who coordinates Annandale High's mentor program. "One by one, these adults can make a significant difference in the lives of students. One mentor waited two years because he wanted to give back to the Korean community by mentoring a student from the Korean culture. He is now doing just that," Sobel says.

I think there is a great value in being both the mentor and mentee, said parent Judy Miller, who mentored a high school student. "I really think being a mentor helped me to become a better parent. My own kids were proud that I was a mentor at their school, even though they didn't know who my student was. Mentoring let me step out of the shoes of a parent in relating to a teenager. It helped me listen to my own children differently."

Share your professional expertise or your hobby in support of the school.

Many parents are crushed between commitments to work and family. They believe they don't have time to devote to volunteering in the school, and it may be true in the traditional sense. But every parent can find some time to contribute to the school if only in a small way.

One meaningful way to help is lending your professional expertise to the school. Several times in the book, I have mentioned how I used my professional expertise as a communications consultant to help build public support for Annandale High School. It was not a one-way street. I gained valuable professional experience, including organizing grass-roots community outreach, facilitating meetings, and speaking before a variety of groups. My volunteer experiences led directly to writing this book.

There is always a task where your talents and experience would provide a valuable contribution. If you are a computer whiz, help organize a needed database. If you are experienced at writing cogent memos, help write up award nominations for faculty or develop grant applications. Surely you will grow from the experience.

The same goes for hobbies. Annandale High has run a successful golf tournament for the last several years. Many of the parents on the planning committee are golf enthusiasts who enjoy organizing the tournament as much as playing in it.

Annandale parent Jennifer Van Pernis, who works in theatrical design, offered to help her son's first grade teacher with a play. She felt the teachers and principal had been very responsive to a concern she had with her son and she wanted to give back to the school. Over the years, volunteering in her son's classroom led to multigrade productions at the elementary and later at the middle school. Several of the students involved in those plays went on to study theater performance and production in college. These days, Van Pernis, the PTA president at Annandale High, is often greeted by high schoolers who fondly remember their roles in those productions.

Help to break down myths about diverse schools by sharing your positive experiences with friends and neighbors.

With myths abounding about diverse schools, it is critical for parents in diverse schools to openly share their positive stories. Parent Liz Segal says she has learned to be assertive in the neighborhood, after falling prey to some of the myths herself before personally investigating Annandale High:

> It is now easy for me, once a quiet, introverted face in the crowd, to challenge a neighbor who succumbs to repeating stereotypical rumors or assumptions about our school. I have been known to call parents who I have heard are hesitating about sending their child to Annandale and keep them on the phone for an hour explaining everything that is good about the high school. I urge them to speak to other parents and students who are actually at our school, rather than listening to inaccurate comments of people without firsthand knowledge.

At Annandale we've learned that we must be aggressive in putting forth the truth. We call reporters who write misleading stories about the school or other diverse schools. We write letters to the editor. When I had an op-ed piece published about the strengths of diverse schools in *USA Today,* the high school PTA distributed it to the principals and PTA leaders in all the elementary and middle schools that feed into our school so they could share the message with their parents. One mother of an Annandale High student told me, her voice cracking with emotion, that it captured all the things she had been trying to explain. She told me she was copying the article to send to neighbors "who just don't get it."

The bottom line for parents is that they must open their eyes to the amazing opportunities for growth, for themselves as well as their children, provided by diverse schools. When you become an active member of a diverse school community, you find ways to strengthen the community as a whole and you, as a part of that whole, are enriched.

NOTES

1. Ivy H. Lovelady, "The Day the Mill Closed," *Educational Leadership* 50, no.1 (September 1992): 55.
2. Anne Henderson and Karen L. Mapp, *A New Wave of Evidence.*

20

STUDENTS: WHAT IT'S ALL ABOUT

Prejudices, it is well known, are most difficult to eradicate from the heart whose soil has never been loosened or fertilized by education: they grow there, firm as weeds among stones.

—Charlotte Brontë, *The Quotable Woman*[1]

Schools exist for the sole purpose of educating our youth. All the adults involved in the school system, from the administrators and teachers to the parents, are there to make sure students are learning and growing.

Adults can only do so much, however. There is a point at which students must take responsibility for their own growth and development. When adults have done their jobs—when students are provided with challenging educational opportunities, when barriers are removed, when teachers and administrators are encouraging and supportive—personal growth rests on the shoulders of the student.

It is clearly within a student's own power to take advantage of the unique opportunities available in a diverse school and participate in building a strong, unified student body. Will the student seek out only those who are similar in background and experience, setting up walls to keep out those who look, sound, or think differently? Or will the student be open to learning from peers who may challenge him to expand his horizons?

For students lucky enough to attend well-run diverse schools at a young age, the question often is moot. When I ask eight- or ten-year olds from these schools about the mix of kids in their classrooms, they usually give me a blank stare. They don't see any distinction among the students in their classrooms. Roni Silverstein talks about the time her adolescent son Michael came to help her with an after-school program in the diverse school where she is assistant principal. Michael, who has pale white skin, came with his best friend Darrell, a dark-skinned African American. As the older boys were leaving, one of the second graders asked, "Are you brothers?"

One parent from a diverse school in the Brandywine District of Delaware, wrote me of her child's birthday party when he was in second grade. "I took a look at the list of kids my son wanted to invite to his birthday party. About one third of his classmates were from 'minority' backgrounds. Sure enough the list of kids he wanted to invite was also about one third." She was pleased to see her son's openness remained much the same as he grew older. "For his last birthday, he was allowed to invite a few kids to a basketball game. Two of the five kids were 'minorities,' so things haven't changed," wrote the parent.

If interaction with peers of different backgrounds is limited during early childhood, the situation gets more complex. Misconceptions and distrust based on lack of exposure can result. In some diverse secondary schools, there is a clear separation between races and ethnic groups. You hear it in student language: "They are winning all the awards," "They took over the football team," "How could they have won the school election?" You see the separation in the halls and in the cafeteria. At school dances, the different groups hang out in separate corners of the gym.

In strong diverse schools, however, students respect one another as individuals. Eventually, they stop viewing each other based on their background and just see fellow classmates. Alice Donlan who attended Stuart High in Fairfax County along with students from seventy nations notes that going to a school like Stuart actually helps you to move beyond diversity. "Stuart faculty really drummed into us the strength of diversity. But at the end of the day, we realized the whole point is that diversity doesn't matter. They are just people. It doesn't matter where they are from; they are just human beings," Donlan says.

When students move beyond fear and mistrust of those who are different and learn to value one another as individuals, they begin seeing the similarities and respecting the differences. That's when a school community flourishes.

There are a number of steps students can take to contribute to the development of a healthy diverse community of students:

Truly listen to students whose ideas are different from your own.

"I enjoy going to a diverse school because you get to learn about other people—where they came from, what they believe in, why they believe in it. The world itself is so diverse, this just strengthens your view of the world," says Ayobamidele Odejimi, a student at Annandale High. Odejimi was born in the United States and lived in Nigeria for a year. "I don't think Americans realize how close-minded and ignorant we are to the world. We need to take advantage of the opportunities to learn more about other people," he says.

Taylor Butler attends Murrah High School in Jackson, Mississippi, a community where middle-class parents banded together to preserve the economic and racial diversity of the public schools. Butler says that one of the strengths of her school is that during class discussions, students listen to the ideas of others, even if they are challenging. "It's one thing to believe things if they are facts and another if they are opinion. In my high school, anyone can be right. You can respect and love and hate another person all at the same time, depending on how what they say relates to your personal beliefs. The discussion makes you a much more intelligent person."

Butler believes that diversity has many meanings. "Economic, racial, social, and religious background all contribute to how a person thinks. The world is a lot bigger than one little school. Students here are open to the real world as it influences the community of our school," she says.

Get out of your comfort zone—put yourself in situations where everyone does not act and think as you do.

"Definitely listening and having an open mind," are the ways to take advantage of a diverse student body, says Sharon Greenbaum of Concord High School in Delaware's Brandywine District. "It's important to not look away from situations where people are different. Seeing people from different backgrounds, wanting to get to know them, to understand them—it makes you a more well-balanced person all around," says Greenbaum who was the student representative on the Brandywine School Board.

Greenbaum took part in Concord High's Leader Corps, a leadership development and team-building initiative. The program began with a retreat in the fall. "It brought people from diverse backgrounds together so we could come back and serve the school and do community service," Greenbaum said. "It changed my outlook on what could be done within a school." She's proud of some of the Leader Corps projects, such as a Family Fun Day for the community. But she also feels she's grown from the experiences of working with so many different students. "School isn't just about going to class, it's also about meeting other people, learning with them and becoming a better person because of who you are surrounded with. We walk down the hall and talk to one another, respect one another, care for one another."

Participate in extracurricular activities, where people of different backgrounds come together with a common goal.

Maybe it's the basketball team, maybe it's the school play, perhaps the school paper. Whatever your interest, as Nike says, just do it. By joining in extracurricular activities, students increase opportunities to meet people from different backgrounds.

"My best experience in high school was being involved," says Taylor Butler. "If you get involved in even one thing, you feel as if you are part of a group. Even if you just come and hang out with the other people, it's worth it." At Butler's high school in Jackson, Mississippi, the school offers "club day" twice a month during activity period, with students able to suggest new clubs. "If it is a productive, positive idea, it will be honored," she says.

Help other students by serving as a student leader, tutor, peer mediator, or mentor.

While adults are there to teach and guide students, there are many opportunities for students to take personal responsibility to build a strong diverse community. Peer mediation programs have been a valuable asset in many diverse schools. With students from many different backgrounds and experiences coming together in one school, misunderstandings can easily escalate into violence if students are not provided with alternative ways of handling the disagreement. Peer mediation empowers students themselves to be the peacemakers in the school.

Annandale High's peer mediation program builds on the foundation of similar programs in the diverse middle schools that feed into it. "We help students solve programs before they can become fights," says student mediator Danni Rumber. "It's easier for students to talk to someone who is a peer than having to talk to an authority figure."

"This program gives the students a sense of ownership of the school," says faculty advisor Lori Barb. Student mediators are involved in helping solve a variety of problems. Sometimes they simply meet with a student and become a mentor and friend, helping work out a problem, perhaps with a teacher. Other times they deal with serious conflicts, sometimes along racial lines. A recent incident involved a student from a Central American country and one from an African nation, both of whom were just learning English. "There was a total misunderstanding interpreting what one student had said," says Barb. "Discussions can get pretty hot as kids defend themselves and where they are from." But at the end of the mediation session, when the students could understand how the communication broke down, the anger was deflated and the kids were even joking a little about it, Barb says.

Annandale's advanced mediation class includes volunteer hours in the community. This year, the students helped straighten up the physical education facilities of a child-care center for low-income parents and cleaned out border space at a nearby veterinary clinic. Barb says activities like this help build the strong community support that Annandale High enjoys.

Invite friends to your family, cultural, or religious celebrations. Express an interest in joining them for a similar experience.
Students in diverse schools enjoy rare opportunities to expand their appreciation of other cultures by sharing in the celebrations and commemorations of their friends. While religious and cultural traditions can be very personal, they can also be of great value in teaching the appreciation of differences if they are shared with respectful friends.

I've witnessed the enlightenment of students who explore the rich heritage of friends, and the fun they have as they see similarities and differences among their traditions. I hear students talk about attending a

Quinceañera or Bat Mitzvah or Confirmation—coming of age ceremonies in different cultures and faiths. I hear them share stories of what they eat, or aren't permitted to eat, on various holidays. They talk about the connection between Communion wafers, part of Christian religious ceremony, and matzah, eaten by Jews at Passover. Students are surprised at the similarities between the precepts of *halal* (Muslim) and kosher (Jewish) dietary laws. After attending different religious services, they discuss whose head is covered, who stands, who bows, who kneels. What language did they hear during the services? Latin? Hebrew? Sanskrit?

Learning extends beyond the classroom or even the school grounds. Sometimes minds are expanded most in kitchens, living rooms, and houses of worship where people are welcomed as guests.

Champion the message of diverse schools.

Sometimes you need to take a stand in support of your school. Dispelling the myths about diverse schools is the job of everyone who understands the benefits of attending a diverse school. Students in the Brandywine District in Delaware stood up next to the adults in the community to support the strength of their schools, as they were being threatened by a new state law, the Neighborhood Schools Act, which would have created schools largely defined by race and income. Kate Bradley from Concord High School spoke at several school district meetings and the state school board meeting. Her words made a lasting impression on everyone who heard them:

> Yelana Bluestein. Dominic Rivera. Latifa Williams. Enrique Nieves. Albert Brown. Beki Bartow. Morgan Gregg. These people are black, white, Hispanic, Christian, Jewish. These are people that I consider my friends. These are also people that I would never have met if Neighborhood Schooling were in effect today. My name is Kate Bradley; I am a senior at Concord High School, and I am pissed. Under Neighborhood Schooling, the children of the Brandywine School District, and other districts in Delaware will grow up never knowing the different and important aspects of other cultures and races. . . . The senior class at Concord High School had an assembly to discuss this law. Many of us were outraged. "Why?" you ask? Because it basically comes down to the fact that we are going back to the 1950s when schools were separated largely by race and wealth. Jessica Blum, a fellow student, and I were so upset that we went to Dr.

Morton and asked her if there was anything that we could do, like protest or conduct a survey. Jess and I came up with the idea to do a mock election among the members of the senior class to find out everyone's opinion. We used the same ballot that was used in the Brandywine School District vote a few months ago. We put it together. We tallied the votes. And we found that of 175 members of the senior class, only seven students supported this law.

Our biggest question is, why did it take so long for someone to ask the students? The majority of us were not even aware that this law was even being discussed until the assembly. We are the ones being affected. Our futures are at stake here. We should have been included in the discussions and the debates right from the beginning, not after the fact. We also want to know what is wrong with the way things are now. We are happy with the current attendance boundaries, so why do they need to be changed?

A lot of you are probably wondering why I care. I'm a senior. I'll be out of here next year. But I am not fighting this law for me. I am fighting this law for my little sister, Morgan. She is only one year old. I am afraid that when this law goes into effect, she will never have the chance to get to know people of different races and creeds. She will never have a Latifa to turn to when she has a fashion crisis. And she will never have an Enrique to turn to when her boyfriend is acting like a jerk. And I'll be damned if I let that happen.

Students who are open to new experiences and new perspectives can gain wisdom far beyond book knowledge. Those who stay within the protected comfort zone of people who simply reflect themselves limit their learning and personal growth. "Living is half of learning," says student Taylor Butler. "If you go to a school with kids only like you because it is comfortable and safe, and everything is perfect, and your pictures always turn out right, good luck finding that 'bubble world' when you graduate. The world is big and different and diverse, and that's why we're all here."

NOTE

1. Charlotte Brontë. *The Quotable Woman* (Philadelphia: Running Press, 1991).

21

COMMUNITY MEMBERS:
CLOSING THE LOOP

Until we go back to thinking about school as the totality of the environment in which a child grows up, we can expect no deep changes. Change requires a community—people living and working together, assuming some common responsibility of something that's of deep concern and interest to all of them, their children.

—Peter Senge, "Rethinking and Co-Creating Schools,"[1]

A strong school is at the heart of a community. Americans overwhelmingly cite public schools as the most important local institution—at least five times more often than citing churches, hospitals, and libraries. Individuals frequently define the communities they live in by their neighborhood public schools.[2] In a multicultural community, the school can bring people together like no other institution.

The point has been made repeatedly—strong schools don't just happen. They take proactive leaders, committed educators, supportive parents, open-minded students, *and* involved community members. There are never enough resources for a public school, especially a school that includes students from a variety of races, ethnic backgrounds, and socioeconomic groups. The community can provide crucial support that validates the work of the educators and buoys students. Community members can support their schools in a number of ways:

Visit your neighborhood schools to get firsthand knowledge, and be a source of accurate information.

Community leaders need to be knowledgeable about the primary institution of the community—the local school. That means community members can't depend on what they heard from a neighbor who has a nephew whose friend attended the school ten years ago. The importance of a positive community "buzz" about the school can't be overemphasized. Many families choose a neighborhood to move into, or out of, based on what they hear from their dentist or their business colleagues at the Chamber of Commerce. The myths surrounding diverse schools will only dissipate when the entire community moves beyond them and speaks from knowledge.

"It is stunning what people come to believe when they don't have broader experiences," says Beverley Baxter, a business leader in the Brandywine District of Delaware. Baxter says the "Principal for a Day" program, coordinated by the Delaware State Chamber of Commerce, opens the eyes of many business leaders to what is really going on in today's public schools. The program pairs business leaders with a school where they spend the day with the school principal to get firsthand experience. "One of my colleagues who had attended parochial schools, sent all of his children to parochial schools, and had never even been in a public school, was stunned by his experience. He marveled that the school he visited was 'just like a parochial school'—the kids were orderly in the halls, the lockers didn't have graffiti all over them, the students were busy learning, and the principal 'had that place running just like a nun!'" Baxter says. Instead of having the media determine his view of public schools, this business leader now knows the reality.

Provide resources that support learning.

Learning is not as simple as assigning a student to a teacher. Many factors inhibit student development. California's Chula Vista School District collaborates with a wide mix of community organizations, including social service agencies, hospitals, government, and businesses. "We're creating family capacity," says Superintendent Libia Gil who views "the entire community as a resource for learning."

One major partnership in Chula Vista brings together the health care community and the education community. At a meeting of the South

Bay Human Services Council, local hospitals reported a high number of uninsured children coming to emergency rooms for their primary health care. School officials found that the neighborhood schools attended by these same students were experiencing a high rate of absenteeism, a problem closely linked to student achievement. With the goal of caring for these interlocking health and education needs, the Spirit of Caring Mobile Health Care Clinic was born. The clinic travels to five elementary schools each week to provide free medical services. This collaborative project between the school district, Sharp Chula Vista Medical Center, Scripps Memorial Hospital Chula Vista, and the City of Chula Vista has reduced absenteeism and cut emergency room visits, leaving students the beneficiaries.

Share your business skills and resources with a school.

It started as a simple concept. Instead of racking their brains to find new items to buy their clients as thank-you gifts during the holidays, Mark and Merrill Shugoll decided to make a donation from Shugoll Research to charity in the name of their clients. The clients of the Bethesda, Maryland, marketing research firm wholeheartedly supported the concept.

The arts community had already been a particular cause of the Shugolls and they began directing some of the donations on behalf of their clients to local theaters in the nearby Washington, D.C., area. Then they began looking more broadly at ways to support the arts. They saw their own children enriched by attending theater and musical performances. They also realized that many other children did not have those opportunities, particularly as cultural school trips were being cut out of budgets. As researchers themselves, the Shugolls were also mindful of the same data that worries the arts community; that theater-goers are an aging population.

The Shugolls decided a partnership between a school and an arts organization would benefit everyone. An active volunteer leader in the arts community, Mark worked fervently to link the new arts center at nearby George Mason University with his neighborhood elementary school, Columbia Elementary in Annandale, Virginia. Under the partnership he helped develop, each class at Columbia adopted an artist. Performers, including nationally known talent such as the Alvin Ailey Dance Company, opera star Heidi Grant Murphy, and the Dance Theater of Senegal, were frequent visitors to the school. Students spent time at the arts center, visiting with artists and watching performances. Mark could see his love of theater spreading to a new young audience. He organized theater trips for the elementary, middle, and high school students to the Kennedy Center for the Performing Arts in Washington, D.C., and other nearby venues. Shugoll Research hired the buses and underwrote the cost of tickets. The program continued to build, as Mark Shugoll called on his personal contacts in the arts community to plan extraordinary free evening events called *ArtSpeak!*, where artists regularly come into the auditorium of the local middle school for discussions with students of every age and their parents. With Mark's help, the students dialogued with numerous nationally renowned artists including choreographer and actor Maurice Hines, composers Marvin Hamlisch and Stephen Schwartz, and theater performers Sally Mayes, Kristin Chenowith, and Brian Stokes Mitchell.

The Shugolls have also lent their support directly to arts programs at Annandale High School, with Shugoll Research underwriting the cost of performance space for the chorus program's "Broadway Desserts." The firm also took steps that broadened student opportunities for selection in the high school's highly competitive top choruses by starting a fund to subsidize private student voice lessons. Shugoll Research's exemplary efforts have been recognized not only by the local Annandale Community Coalition, but by the *Washington Post*, which recognized them for Innovative Leadership in the Theatre and Community, and by the Business Committee for the Arts and *Forbes Magazine*, which presented the firm with its national Innovation Award.

Volunteer in the school and encourage your employees and coworkers to become involved.

There are many opportunities to share your knowledge and skills with students. "Chess in the Schools" is a national program that brings chess masters into schools to work with the students. At Dallas' Walnut Hill Elementary School, the third graders were thrilled when they placed third in a chess competition thanks to the coaching of weekly chess tutor Stephen Gerzadowicz. He was equally delighted by their success.

Chess masters may be rare, but a multitude of business people have something to offer their local schools and they learn lessons in the process. You can hear the enthusiasm when Winnie McGarty of Xerox Corporation talks about mentoring a student at Annandale High:

> I have told everyone what a wonderful experience being a mentor has been. My mentee is one of the sweetest girls in the world. We meet once a week and both of us look forward to each and every meeting. We have shared family pictures, talked about the good things she is doing through a service organization, talked about grades and how she is working to improve on them. Most important we talk every week about how the choices she is making now, both academically and personally, affect her future. I plan on bringing her to work, showing her the technology and giving her a couple of ideas regarding career possibilities. It is absolutely a highlight of my week to be with her as a mentor.

"People don't realize the value that they themselves get from being a mentor," says McGarty. "If you help someone out, the company wins and the individual wins. The company gains because the employee is more motivated. This kind of relationship helps people to feel they are valued, and this transposes into their work." McGarty notes this extra inspiration is important in today's work environment where cutbacks and reduced budgets require employees to work harder than they ever have.

"This also reflects back on my personal life and everyone I interact with," says McGarty. "I feel myself light up when I start talking about my mentee." McGarty recognizes it is hard to make time for a commitment like this, but the positive results multiply. "The mentor gains, the company gains, the student gains, the school gains, and the whole community gains." She has organized her office, a small branch of Xerox Corporation in McLean, Virginia, to support Annandale High's mentoring program. Many now share her enthusiasm.

There are countless ways to make a meaningful contribution to a school that don't involve money or the resources of a huge corporation. Priceless contributions include helping out with the boys soccer team or volunteering for career day at the middle school or reading to the first graders. Just by coming into the school, community volunteers let students know that they feel education is important. The students get the opportunity to interact with a caring adult beyond their family and teacher. And the volunteers receive the matchless gift of making a difference in the life of a child.

NOTES

1. Peter Senge, "Rethinking and Co-Creating Schools," *Community Development Journal* 2, no. 3 (Summer 2001): 14–17.

2. *Action for All: The Public's Responsibility for Public Education* (Washington, D.C.: Public Education Network, 2001).

"Christmas Deer," by Dennis Bundu

CONCLUSION

Every day, parents agonize over decisions about educating their children. For middle class parents who have the luxury of moving, they seek neighborhoods with "good schools." Many who grew up in white middle-class communities have happy memories of their childhood. Having no exposure to any other type of community, they seek the comfort of what they know, where their view of the world will be reinforced.

Even if they consider diverse schools for their children, they hear disturbing messages. Standardized test scores in schools with racial and ethnic minorities are often lower that the white middle-class schools, so they must be academically inferior. They see reports in the media about problems in a few schools outside the white suburbs and generalize these to all schools with diverse populations. They ignore the reports about problems in middle-class suburban schools because their limited life experiences tell them that kids in those schools are the ones who come from good families who care, so the problems must be the exceptions.

If these parents consider a diverse school, neighbors quickly point out the foolishness of that idea. "You wouldn't send your child to *that* school," says the mother who moved into an all-white neighborhood. "You know, it's not what it used to be," says the father whose son graduated in 1980.

Real estate agents push properties with "good schools," hiking up the price of homes in these predominantly white neighborhoods.

It's a vicious cycle that plays itself out in communities all over America. It's a cycle based on myths that have somehow become ingrained in American culture, resulting in faulty logic that leads parents to make uninformed decisions. They deprive their children of the unique educational environment that can only be found in our diverse public schools. What a pity.

But now you understand the myths about diverse schools and you know the realities. Now you know how a strong diverse school can enrich every student, teacher, administrator, parent, and community member. Now you know what it takes to run a strong diverse school. Now you know your unique and valuable part in strengthening these educational fields of dreams.

The questions remain. Will you read this book and say that the message applies to some other schools somewhere else, not the diverse ones near you? Will you find that your role as educator, parent, or student is "better" in an environment where everyone is your mirror image? Or will you take personal responsibility for finding out the truth, debunking the myths, and strengthening diverse schools? I'm here to tell you it's worth every ounce of effort. Our entire family is grateful for the lessons taught to us by Annandale High School, lessons that multiply by guiding us in the way we live our lives every day.

Let's redefine "good schools" and reap the rich harvest of our diverse schools.

EPILOGUE

I was visiting my son Alex at college, having lunch in a park near his dorm with a few of his friends. Nathan was telling us about his "alternative spring break" program, where he spent a week in the South Bronx, helping at an inner-city elementary school with a population almost exclusively African American and Hispanic. "It gave me insight into the reality of another school. The kids were just regular kids—but the experiences that they consider 'normal' were things that I would never think were. The important thing was to be there and experience it firsthand." Nathan didn't expect to feel as comfortable as he did in the neighborhood, even when he played a pickup basketball game on a neighborhood court. "I was happy and really surprised that I wasn't treated like 'the white guy.'"

Pondering what Nathan had said, another friend thought about her own experiences. She, like Nathan, had spent her whole life with people like herself—middle-class white. "I think I'm open-minded, but how do you know if you've never had the opportunity to test it?" she said. Her comments made me think about our responsibility as parents not only to provide for our children's comfort, but to encourage them to get out of that comfort zone from time to time.

I recognize that not everyone has the opportunity to attend a well-run diverse school. It doesn't mean there are no options for personal interactions with people of other races and ethnicities. It just means you have to make a serious effort to seek out those opportunities.

If you are the parent of school-age children, I urge you to do whatever you can to expose your children to people who will broaden their perspective on life. Look for classes or enrichment programs that will attract people from different backgrounds; encourage them to join a club or sports team with kids from outside your neighborhood; help your children take part in regional or state events that take them into new neighborhoods; find a summer program, possibly in another part of the country, that will expose your children to new ideas and new people.

There are incredible opportunities all around us. My son took part in a year-long leadership program for Jewish and African American teenagers, Operation Understanding, in which they studied each other's history and culture and had intensive discussions to gain insights into the historic and current relationship between their two peoples. During July they took a month-long bus trip together to talk with key individuals and visit sites that were instrumental in the Civil Rights movement. For many students on that bus—black and white—this was their first experience outside their largely segregated public and private schools. It changed every one of them for life. This remarkable program, which operates in several cities, is completely free to the participants, supported by contributions from individuals and foundations.

While finding an experience for your own child is valuable, you can also be a force for expanding the horizons of many students in your community. Work with your school administration to find ways for students to interact with peers of different backgrounds on a regular basis. Joe Cirasuolo, a past president of the American Association for School Administrators who is superintendent of schools in Wallingford, Connecticut, is committed to increasing opportunities for the students in his predominantly white schools. He supports several programs that intermix students from the inner-city schools of New Haven with his students.

"If we limit our students interactions, we allow them to grow up crippled, cut off from relating to a majority of the human race," Cirasuolo states. "Every interaction helps us grow and become better human beings."

Cirasuolo recounts a story of the girls' cross-country team from one of his schools that was to run through the streets of New Haven in a meet with a team from an inner-city school. When his students got off the bus in the city, they were immediately greeted by adults and students from New Haven who assured them that the streets were secured and safe, and they realized this was an issue for the students at both schools. The Wallingford team went on to beat the New Haven team, and the suburban girls were a little apprehensive about the reaction of the city team. Instead of what the Wallingford girls feared might happen, the New Haven team had prepared a picnic where both teams could celebrate the event. "All the things I thought about the kids from New Haven were not true," a member of the Wallingford team told Cirasuolo.

Mary Barter, who has led school districts in several parts of the country, says there are many ways to increase opportunities for students to be exposed to people from other backgrounds. She started a leadership program for fifth grade girls at the Three Village Central School District in Stony Brook, on New York's Long Island. Students from the district's five elementary schools participated, as well as fifth grade girls from seven other school districts on Long Island, bringing together girls from a wide variety of backgrounds. "I wanted them to know that leadership comes in all shapes and forms," she says. Among the group's activities was a trip to New York City so the girls could be exposed to a broader mix of people.

Certainly opportunities for exposure to other cultures in an academic setting don't end when a student leaves for college. Jimmy Kim, a Korean-American who graduated from a high school that was largely white, was determined to expand his base when he went to the University of Virginia, which itself is predominantly white. "I didn't go to college just to meet middle-class white and Asian students," Kim says. "I consciously made an effort to go outside my social group." One of his strategies was to take a class in Black Writers in America. "I learned a ton in that class, not only from the material but also from the students," Kim says. "Probably the most important thing I learned is that not all white students think alike and not all black students think alike. If you weren't involved in that discourse, you might think that the statistics about both races apply to everyone." Kim earned a B.S. and M.A. at the university, taught in a very diverse middle school and then earned his doctorate at the Harvard School of Education, researching issues relating to minority achievement.

There are a variety of programs for college-age students aimed at broadening the horizons of our future leaders. Many colleges offer alternative spring break programs like the one Nathan Sisterson joined. The programs involve teams of students in community-based service projects, giving them opportunities to understand the issues faced in communities far different than their own. Nathan said his time in the South Bronx gave him a new perspective. Every night his group would reflect on their experiences. "A lot of what I got out of this experience was from the dialogue with Tiffany, one of the students in my group who grew up in South Chicago. She challenged the rest of the group all the time," Nathan says. "I just see things from a different angle now. Things that might not have offended me before do now. I feel it is important to speak out," he said.

It is important that we all—children and adults alike—gain personal knowledge of life beyond our own. We all grow from the experience of seeing life from other perspectives. As numerous people said to me during interviews for this book, you don't really know what you believe in until someone questions you. It's only by hearing someone with different ideas that you begin to dig deep inside to contemplate whether the belief is something you affirm or something you are simply parroting back based on things you've been told. It's a healthy process.

Our world today demands that we see beyond our own home and our carefully chosen friends and neighbors, particularly if they are all of the same race, ethnicity, and social class as we. We can't close our eyes to other experiences and other realities. This is especially true for our children. We owe it to them to give them the gift of expanding beyond their comfort zone. It's not always easy for them, or you. But their lives will be enriched immeasurably. And you will give them the valuable tools they'll need to thrive in the exciting multicultural world in which they live.

BIBLIOGRAPHY

Action for All: The Public's Responsibility for Public Education. Washington, D.C.: Public Education Network, 2001.

Bacon, Beth. "Increasing Safety in America's Public Schools." *Lessons from the Field* 6 (April 2001), Public Education Network.

Banks, James A. "Educating for Diversity." *Educational Leadership* 51, no. 8 (May 1994).

Banks, James A., and Cherry A. McGee. *The Handbook of Research on Multicultural Education.* New York: Jossey-Bass, 2001.

Berg, Ellen. "Teaching Students How to Give the Man What He Wants." www.middleweb.com/mw/msdiaries/01-02wklydiaries/EB18.html [accessed 15 June 2002].

Blum, R. W., and P. Mann Rinehart. *Reducing the Risk: Connections That Make a Difference in the Lives of Youth.* Minneapolis: Division of General Pediatrics and Adolescent Health, University of Minnesota, 1998.

Blum, R. W., and C. A. McNeely. *Improving the Odds: The Untapped Power of Schools to Improve the Health of Teens.* Minneapolis: Center for Adolescent Health and Development, University of Minnesota, 2000.

Bredhoff & Kaiser, P.L.L.C. *The Benefits of a Racially-Diverse Student Body in Elementary/Secondary Education.* Washington, D.C.: National Education Association, 1999.

Brontë, Charlotte. *The Quotable Woman.* Philadelphia: Running Press, 1991.

Chisholm, Shirley. *A Special Relationship: Our Teachers and How We Learned*, ed. John C. Board. Wainscott, N.Y.: Pushcart Press, 1991.

Collier, Virginia. "Age and Rate of Acquisition of Second Language for Academic Purposes." *TESOL Quarterly* 21, no. 4 (1987): 617–41.

Darden, Edwin C., Arthur L. Coleman, and Scott R. Palmer. *From Desegregation to Diversity: A School District's Self-Assessment Guide on Race, Student Assignment and the Law*. Washington, D.C.: National School Boards Association, 2002.

"Demographic Data from National Center for Educational Statistics." nces.ed.gov/nceskids/index.html [accessed 15 June 2002].

Domenech, Daniel A. "My Stakes Well Done." *School Administrator* 57, no. 11 (December 2000), 14–19.

Erickson, Donna. "Geometry Teacher's 'Project Quilt Day' Leads to 'More Than I Bargained For!'" *Alpha Delta KAPPAN* (December 2000): 21–23.

Extracurricular Participation and Student Engagement. National Center for Education Statistics, U.S. Department of Education, June 1995.

Farkas, Steve, Jean Johnson, Ann Duffett, and Tony Foleno. *Trying to Stay Ahead of the Game*, Washington D.C.: Public Agenda, 2001.

Finders, Margaret, and Cynthia Lewis. "Why Some Parents Don't Come to School." *Educational Leadership* 51, no. 8 (May 1994): 50–52.

Gil, Libia, and Dennis M. Doyle. "A District Responds: Embracing Diversity." *State Education Standard* (Winter 2002): 20–25.

Gurin, Patricia. "The Compelling Need for Diversity in Higher Education." Expert testimony in *Gratz et al. v. Bollinger et al.* (No. 97-75231 E.D. Mich., filed 1997; and No. 97-75972 E.D. Mich., filed 1997), 1999.

Harris, Kathleen Mullan. "Health Risk Behavior among Adolescents in Immigrant Families." Paper presented at the Urban Seminar Series on Children's Health and Safety, Harvard University, 2–3 December 1999.

Henderson, Anne, and Karen L. Mapp. *A New Wave of Evidence: The Impact of School, Family, and Community Connections on Student Achievement*. Austin Tex.: Southwest Educational Development Laboratory, 2002.

Henze, Rosemary C. *Leading for Diversity: How School Leaders Achieve Racial and Ethnic Harmony*. Santa Cruz: Center for Research on Education, Diversity & Excellence, University of California at Santa Cruz, June 2000.

Hodgkinson, Harold. "Educational Demographics: What Teachers Should Know." *Educational Leadership* 58, no. 4 (December 2000/January 2001).

hooks, bell. *Teaching to Transgress: Education as the Practice of Freedom*. New York: Routledge, 1994.

Houston, Paul. "Superintendents for the 21st Century: It's Not Just a Job, It's a Calling." *Kappan Magazine* 82, no. 6 (February 2001): 428–33.

Immerwahr, John, with Tony Foleno. "Great Expectations: How the Public and Parents—White, African American and Hispanic—View Higher Education." *Public Agenda* (May 2000): 4.

The Impact of Racial and Ethnic Diversity on Educational Outcomes, Cambridge, MA, School District. Cambridge, Mass.: Civil Rights Project, Harvard University, 2002.

Johnson, Jean. "Will Parents and Teachers Get on the Bandwagon to Reduce School Size?" *Phi Delta Kappan* 83, no. 5 (January 2002): 353–56.

Kahlenberg, Richard. *All Together Now.* Washington, D.C.: Brookings Institution Press, 2001.

Kohn, Alfie. *The Schools Our Children Deserve.* New York: Houghton Mifflin, 1999.

Kurlaender, Michael, and John T. Yun. "Is Diversity a Compelling Educational Interest? Evidence from Metropolitan Louisville." In *Diversity Challenged*, ed. Gary Orfield. Cambridge, Mass.: Harvard Education Publishing Group, 2001.

Lareau, Annette, and Erin McNamara Horvat. "Moments of Social Inclusion and Exclusion: Race, Class and Cultural Capital in Family-Social Relationships." *Sociology of Education* 72 (January 1999): 37–53.

Lovelady, Ivy H. "The Day the Mill Closed." *Educational Leadership* 50, no. 1 (September 1992): 55.

Martin, Bill Jr. *Knots on a Counting Rope.* New York: Holt, 1987.

Midobuche, Eva. "Respect in the Classroom: Reflections of a Mexican–American Educator." *Educational Leadership* 56, no. 7 (April 1999): 80–82.

Miller, Walter B. *The Growth of Youth Gang Problems in the United States: 1970–98.* Washington, D.C.: Office of Juvenile Justice and Delinquency Prevention, U.S. Department of Justice, 2001.

National Center for Educational Statistics. "A Time Line of Recent School Shootings." *Infoplease.com, Learning Network.* infoplease.com/ipa/A0777958.html [accessed 15 June 2002].

"The National Cross-Site Evaluation of High-Risk Youth Programs." Center for Substance Abuse Prevention, Substance Abuse and Mental Health Services Administration, DHHS Publication No. SMA-25-01: Rockville, Md., 2002.

Nieto, Sonia. "What Does It Mean to Affirm Diversity?" *School Administrator* 56, no. 5 (May 1999): 6–7.

Noguera, Pedro. "Confronting the Challenge of Diversity." *School Administrator* 56, no. 5 (May 1999): 16–18.

Nuridden, Naeema. "Cultural Diversity and the Schools." *Equity News* (Winter 1999).

Orfield, Gary. ed. *Diversity Challenged.* Cambridge, Mass.: Harvard Education Publishing Group, 2001.

———. "Our Resegregated Schools." *Principal Magazine* 79, no. 5 (May 2000), 6–11.

———. *Schools More Separate: Consequences of a Decade of Resegregation.* Cambridge, Mass.: Civil Rights Project, Harvard University, 2001.

Paige, Rod. "Statement on International Education Week." Issued by the Secretary of Education introducing International Education Week, 12–16 November, 2001. www.ed.gov/offices/OUS/PES/endorsement-10172001.html [accessed 15 June 2002].

Peterson, Kent D., and Terrence E. Deal. "How Leaders Influence the Culture of Schools." *Educational Leadership* 56, no. 1 (September 1998): 28.

Popham, W. James. "Right Task, Wrong Tool." *American School Board Journal* 189, no. 2 (February 2002), 18–22.

Public and Private School Principals in the United States: A Statistical Profile, 1993–94 (NCES 97-455) Washington, D.C.: National Center for Educational Statistics, U.S. Department of Education.

Public Education Network. *Increasing Safety in America's Public Schools: Lessons from the Field.* Washington, D.C.: Author, 2001.

Riley, Richard. "The 21st Century Principal: Opportunities and Challenges. An Interview with U.S. Secretary of Education Richard W. Riley and NAESP Executive Director Vincent L. Ferrandino." *Principal Magazine* 80, no.1 (September 2000), 6–12.

Ruiz-de-Velasco, Jorge, and Michael Fix. *Overlooked and Underserved: Immigrant Children in U.S. Secondary Schools.* Washington, D.C.: Urban Institute, 2001.

Rylant, Cynthia. *The Relatives Came.* New York: Bradbury Press, 1985.

Sacks, Peter. "Predictable Losers in Testing Schemes." *School Administrator* 57, no. 11 (December 2000), 6–9.

Schultz, Bridget, and Dan Keating. "'Gifted' Grow Even in Weak Schools." *Washington Post*, 2 September 2001, 12A.

Schwartz, Wendy. "A Guide to Communicating with Asian American Families." *ERIC Clearinghouse on Urban Education*, New York: Teachers College. ericweb.tc.Columbia.edu/guides/pg2.html [accessed 15 June 2002].

———. "Strategies for Improving the Educational Outcomes of Latinas." *ERIC Clearinghouse on Urban Education*, no. 167. New York: Teachers College, October 2001, EDO-UD-01-6.

Senge, Peter. "Rethinking and Co-Creating Schools." *Community Development Journal* 2, no. 3 (Summer 2001), 14–17.

Swerdlow, Joel L. "Changing America." *National Geographic* (September 2001): 43–61.

Vail, Kathleen. "The Changing Face of Education." *Education Vital Signs*, supplement to *American School Board Journal* 188, no. 12 (December 2001).

Van Derwerker, Mickey, and Roxanne Grossman. "The Truth about SOLs." Paper presented at education-related meetings by Parents across Virginia United to Reform SOLs, 2000.

White-Clark, Renee, and Larry E. Decker. *The "Hard-To-Reach" Parent: Old Challenges, New Insights*, 1996. eric-web.tc.Columbia.edu/families/hard_to_reach/chapter1.html#parent [accessed 15 June 2002].

Wiesel, Elie. *Night*. New York: Bantam, 1982.

Wise, Tim. "School Shootings and White Denial." *AlterNet Online Magazine*. www.alternet.org/story.html?StoryID=10560, 6 March 2001 [accessed 15 June 2002].

"WorkForce Technologies." Parent Satisfaction Survey Report, Fairfax County Public Schools, 14 September 2001.

Youth Violence: A Report of the Surgeon General. Executive Summary. Washington, D.C.: U.S. Department of Health and Human Services (2001): 4–5.

www.ed.gov [accessed 15 June 2002].

www.ed.gov/offices/OUS/PES/endorsement-10172001.html [accessed 15 June 2002].

www.Parents4PublicSchools.com [accessed 15 June 2002].

ABOUT THE AUTHOR

Eileen Gale Kugler has been on the front lines of communication for more than three decades. Her varied background includes working as a journalist, information director for a federal agency, and executive of several nonprofits. In 1992, she founded Kugler Communications, a firm specializing in strategic planning, communications training, and media outreach.

Eileen's interest in diverse schools began more than a decade ago, when her older child entered Annandale High School in Fairfax County, Virginia, a school with students from more than eighty-five nations who speak more than forty languages. Collaborating with school administrators and teachers, Eileen developed and implemented an innovative strategy to bring accurate information about the school to the community, reaching out to young parents, real estate agents, civic associations, and community service organizations. With Eileen's help, the once-negative tone of media coverage changed to one of national and international recognition for the school's achievements. Eileen has won numerous awards for her efforts.

Today, she is a national advocate for diverse schools, speaking and writing on the benefits of a diverse student body, and consulting with school districts.

Eileen lives in Springfield, Virginia, with her husband, Larry. They enjoy the visits of their children, Sara and Alex, who are busy making their own marks on the world. She can be reached at Ekugler@ KuglerCom.com.